NIAGARA

The Falls and the River

An Illustrated History

Kevin Woyce

Photographs by the Author

Also available as an e-book

Website: KevinWoyce.com
Facebook: Kevin Woyce Author
Instagram: @kevinwoyce

CONTENTS

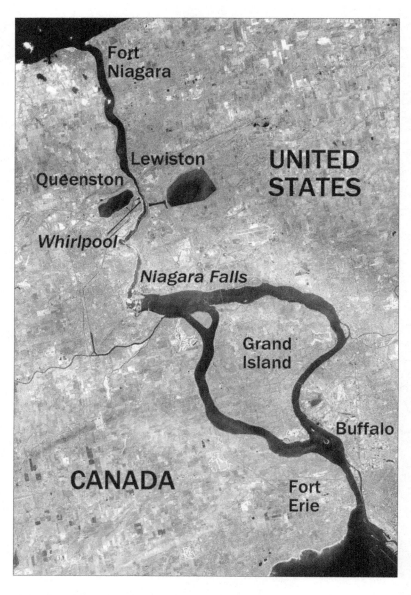

The **Niagara River** (NASA Terra satellite photo, 2001).

Chapter One
Fort Erie and Buffalo

THE NIAGARA RIVER flows north from Lake Erie to Lake Ontario. Because it drops 325 feet in rapids and falls, French explorers took its name from a native phrase meaning "Thunder of Waters."

The thirty-five-mile river has been an international border since 1783, when the American Revolution ended. Its southern stretch—sometimes called the Upper Niagara—separates the Canadian city of Fort Erie from Buffalo, New York.

Fort Erie was established in 1784, by the Loyalists who settled southern Ontario after the Revolution. They named the town for a riverfront fort the British had built twenty years earlier, after winning the French and Indian War (known in Europe as the "Seven Years' War"). Used as a supply depot during the Revolution, the fort was rebuilt, of stone and on higher ground, in the early 1800s.

American troops captured Fort Erie in July 1814. The British tried to retake it in August, with a siege that lasted into the middle of September. More than three thousand men died in the fighting, and the Americans left the fort in ruins when they withdrew to Buffalo in November.

In the late 1930s, Depression relief workers restored the fort to its 1812 appearance. Renamed Old Fort Erie, it was opened to the public as a historic site on July 1, 1939. The battles of 1814 are reenacted every summer on "Siege Weekend," the second weekend in August. Nearby attractions include the 1918 Point Abino Lighthouse, the Town of Fort Erie's lakefront beaches, and the historic Fort Erie Racetrack, built in 1897.

THIRTEEN DUTCH INVESTORS formed the Holland Land Company in the 1780s and bought more than five thousand square miles of western New York (it would all be sold by 1840, and the Company was dissolved in 1846). In 1803, surveyor Joseph Ellicott laid out the town of New Amsterdam, where the Buffalo River flows into Lake Erie. Five years later, the townspeople voted to change their name to The Village of Buffalo, even though there were no bison left in western New York.

Buffalo remained a small town until 1825, when the Erie Canal opened, connecting the Great Lakes to the Hudson River. When the population reached ten thousand in 1832, Buffalo incorporated as a city. By the 1840s, she was "the Queen City," the second largest in the state of New York. In the early 1900s, electricity from Niagara Falls made Buffalo "The City of Lights."

Two hundred and forty thousand of those electric lights decorated the grounds of Buffalo's Pan American Exposition, which ran from May to November 1901 and drew eight million visitors. Forty-four thousand bulbs illuminated the Electric Tower, the Exposition's 390-foot centerpiece. The Tower also had restaurants inside, an observation deck 250 feet above the grounds, and a searchlight on top that was visible from Niagara Falls, twenty miles away.

Vice President Theodore Roosevelt opened the Exposition on May 5, and President William McKinley visited with his wife, Ida, on September 4. McKinley gave a speech the following day that fit well with the Exposition's promise of "commercial well-being and good understanding among the American Republics."

"Who can tell," The President said, "the new thoughts that have been awakened, the ambition fired, and the high achievement that will be wrought through this exposition?"

Tragedy struck the following day. After visiting Niagara Falls, McKinley returned to the Exposition, where he was shot twice by anarchist Leon Czolgosz. Eight days later, McKinley died, and Theodore Roosevelt was sworn in as president. The ceremony was held at the home of Buffalo lawyer and activist Ansley Wilcox, who had helped to preserve Niagara Falls (his mansion is now the Theodore Roosevelt Inaugural National Historic Site). Czolgosz, who said, "I killed the President because he was the enemy of the … good working people," was sentenced to death and electrocuted on October 29, 1901.

Niagara's power did more than light the city—it transformed Buffalo from a nineteenth-century shipping center into a major industrial city. Buffalo mills produced everything from airplanes to wallpaper. From 1901 until 1938, Pierce-Arrow automobiles rolled off the city's assembly line. General Mills was organized in Buffalo, and Nabisco had one of its first plants there. Fisher-Price toys came from Buffalo, along with the first kazoos.

Lincoln, the Emancipator, a 1902 sculpture by Charles Niehaus, commands the south portico of the Buffalo History Museum. President Lincoln visited Buffalo in February 1861, on his way to the White House. Charles Niehaus also carved the marble figures in the Museum's pediment, which was inspired by the Parthenon in Athens, Greece. Six of his statues, including figures of Henry Clay and President James A. Garfield, stand in the United States Capitol's National Statuary Hall.

Though Buffalo's importance as a shipping and manufacturing center has declined since the 1950s, some light manufacturing remains, a few high-tech companies have moved in, and several banks and insurance companies have Buffalo headquarters.

The **Buffalo History Museum** was originally the New York State Building, the only permanent structure raised for the 1901 Pan American Exposition (all the others were made of wood and plaster and were demolished after the fair closed). The Museum houses exhibits on Buffalo's history and industries; reproductions of early shops and businesses; and a carriage that belonged to President Millard Fillmore (one of the founders of the Buffalo Historical Society, and its first president).

The **Albright-Knox Gallery,** designed as a Fine Arts Pavilion for the Pan American Exposition but not completed until 1905, houses a world-famous collection of modern and contemporary art. Along with the nearby Buffalo History Museum, it is located in Delaware Park, which was designed by landscape architects Frederick Law Olmsted and Calvert Vaux. (In the late nineteenth century, Olmsted and Vaux created dozens of urban parks, including New York's Central Park and the Niagara Reservation. In Buffalo, their parks and parkways are maintained by the nonprofit Buffalo Olmsted Parks Conservancy.)

The **Electric Tower** was the centerpiece of the 1901 Pan American Exposition in Buffalo.

Chapter Two
The International Railway Bridge

BY THE EARLY 1850S, businessmen on both sides of the upper Niagara River were calling for a bridge between Buffalo and Fort Erie. Cargo arrived in both cities by railroad but had to be loaded onto ferries for an often-dangerous river crossing. In 1805, Boston lawyer Timothy Bigelow wrote of waiting more than an hour for a "crazy flat-bottom boat" that had "begun to decay." The current is fast, sometimes as high as twelve miles an hour. And though this current is swift enough to prevent the Niagara from freezing, ice begins forming along the shores of Lake Erie as early as November. All winter long, ice drifts into the river, sometimes choking it from shore to shore.

The owners of Canada's Grand Trunk Railway announced plans for an international bridge in 1857. But the ice and the current weren't the only obstacles they faced. Skeptics said the channel was impossible to bridge. Soundings showed the center of the river to be almost fifty feet deep. Some parts of the riverbed were solid rock, but the rest was clay covered with up to ten feet of gravel.

There were also international agreements to be made, but for most of the 1860s, the United States was mired in the Civil War and Reconstruction. So, it was not until May 1870, that American and Canadian interests merged to form the International Bridge Company, which promised a river crossing by the end of 1871. Though the contract was awarded to Gzowski & Company, Canada's most experienced railway builders, construction took two years longer than expected.

Casimir Stanislaus Gzowski was born in 1813, to polish parents residing in Saint Petersburg. He fled Russia in 1830, after taking part in an insurrection against Tsarist rule. Before settling in Canada in 1841, he spent several years as an engineer on the New York and Erie Railroad. He started his own firm in 1853, to build part of the Grand Trunk.

Eight massive piers carry Gzowski's 3,651-foot International Railway Bridge across the Niagara. Built with stone from Canadian quarries, their south faces are pointed to deflect floating ice. Where the riverbank was clay rather than rock, tons of loose gravel had to be moved before the first pilings could be driven. Unusually icy winters slowed the already difficult work, so that the last pier was not completed until July 1873.

Iron trusses were then floated between the piers on pontoons, which were flooded to lower the bridge sections into place. The last link was completed on October 29, 1873, and the bridge opened four days later. Two bridge spans, one over the main channel and one crossing the Black Rock Canal, were designed to swing so large freighters and tankers could pass. Wooden "rest piers" filled with stone supported the ends of these trusses when they were opened. The main channel swing is still used.

The **International Railway Bridge** photographed from Buffalo.

In 1901, larger and stronger trusses were built around the original ironwork, which was then disassembled and removed—all without stopping traffic. An embankment replaced the iron trestle crossing Buffalo's Squaw Island (which separates the Black Rock Canal from the Niagara River), and the pedestrian sidewalk was removed to make room for a second track.

The International Railway Bridge has carried the Grand Trunk, Erie, Great Western, Canadian Southern, New York Central, and several other railroads. On its busiest day—July 10, 1916—264 trains crossed (the modern average is ten to fifteen daily). Because the bridge brought so much business to Fort Erie, part of that city's downtown has been called "Bridgeburg" since 1895.

Chapter Three
The Peace Bridge

IN 1893, INVENTOR ALONZO MATHER proposed building an international harbor at the head of the Niagara River. His plans included a wide bridge carrying trolleys, pedestrians, and carriage lanes between Fort Erie and Buffalo, about a mile south of the International Railway Bridge.

Though few doubted the need for such a bridge, it would never be built. The Canadian government authorized its construction, and Mather bought land on both sides of the river for approaches. The New York legislature voted three times to build the bridge, and Governor Theodore Roosevelt signed a "Mather Bridge Bill" in April 1900.

But Mather wanted his bridge to pay for its own construction and maintenance, by generating electricity from the fast current between its stone piers. He said that with seven waterwheels, each two hundred feet wide, the "Power Bridge" would "make Buffalo the electrical city of the United States." To prove that his ideas were sound, he offered to build the first span at his own expense.

The opportunity never came. Though Mather planned a four-hundred-foot drawbridge span over the river's deepest channel, the Niagara Falls power companies—which made most of their money transmitting electricity to Buffalo—convinced the War Department that the bridge would hinder navigation.

Still, a bridge was needed. Buffalo businessmen Frank Baird and William Eckert, with attorney John Van Allen, formed the Buffalo and Fort Erie Bridge Company in 1919. Edward Payson Lupfer, who had built bridges for the New York Central and the Great Northern, designed a graceful span of six steel arches supported by stone piers (because the Coast Guard regulations required a hundred-foot clearance across the entire width of the Black Rock Canal, he later changed the easternmost arch to a simpler truss). Baird chose the name "Peace Bridge" to celebrate the (mostly) peaceful relations between the United States and Canada since the War of 1812.

Construction began August 17, 1925, and Edward Lupfer drove the first car across on May 13, 1927. The Peace Bridge opened to traffic on the first of June, and the August 7 Opening Ceremonies drew more than a hundred thousand spectators, including Vice President Charles Dawes, New York Governor Al Smith, British Prime Minister Stanley Baldwin, and the Prince of Wales (the future King Edward VIII). An estimated fifty million radio listeners heard the coast-to-coast broadcast, including the first performance of the *Peace Bridge March* by Buffalo composer Emma Herold-Haft.

The Peace Bridge was dedicated to Alonzo Mather, who had sold his land to Baird's company for the same price he had paid for it. In 1940, Mather donated another seventy-five acres and thirty thousand dollars to build Mather Park at the Canadian entrance.

The **Peace Bridge** photographed from Buffalo.

Today, the bridge is one of the busiest US-Canada border crossings, carrying more than six million cars, trucks, and busses every year. Proposals for increasing its capacity have ranged from building a nearly identical bridge alongside to replacing the aging structure with a modern span.

Did you know?

Alonzo Mather, a distant relation of Puritan preacher Cotton Mather (1663-1728), was founder and president of the Mather Stock Car Company. The American Humane Society awarded him a medal in 1883 for designing a livestock railcar in which cattle could eat and drink during transport. The company's 1928 headquarters—a forty-three story, 521-foot skyscraper—was named a Chicago Historic Landmark in 2001; the lower floors are now the River Hotel. Mather lived to ninety-three, received thirty-one patents, and spent his last year designing a single-person, thousand-dollar aircraft.

The United States and Canada issued commemorative postage stamps for the Peace Bridge's fiftieth anniversary in August 1977. For the seventy-fifth anniversary in 2002, a parade of antique automobiles loaned by Buffalo's Pierce-Arrow Museum crossed the bridge; the *Peace Bridge March* was played again, and a ribbon was cut at the border.

The **Buffalo Skyway,** which opened in 1955, is one of Edward Payson Lupfer's later works. Two dozen reinforced concrete piers raise the 1.4-mile roadway a hundred feet or more above the Buffalo waterfront. Many in Buffalo consider the Skyway an unnecessary barrier between the city and Lake Erie and would like to see it demolished. Other groups have suggested transforming it into a bicycle path or a public park. The grain elevator in the background is a reminder of Buffalo's years as a major Great Lakes shipping center.

Chapter Four
Grand Island

TO THE SENECA who hunted and fished there, the Niagara's largest island was *Ga-we-not*, "The Great Island." The French called it *La Grande Île*. Today it is Grand Island, eight miles long and six wide, the fourth largest island in the state of New York.

New York bought Grand Island from the Iroquois in 1815, for a thousand dollars up front and five hundred dollars every June. In 1817, a few families of squatters began building log cabins and cutting down the island's white pines to make barrel staves; the county sheriff and militia drove them out in 1819. Five years later, Mordecai Manuel Noah came from New York City to establish a Jewish city called "Ararat" on 2,555 untamed acres. He laid a cornerstone, which is now in the Buffalo History Museum, but was unable to attract any settlers to the hard-to-reach island.

Lewis Allen was born in Massachusetts but came to Buffalo in 1827 as financial manager for the Western Ensurance Company. In 1833, he negotiated the Boston Lumber Company's purchase of sixteen thousand acres of Grand Island's white pine forests. Allen helped the company build a small town called White Haven, where a steam-powered sawmill reduced the pines to lumber for the shipyards of New York and Boston.

After cutting the white pines, the Lumber Company sold its land to developers, speculators, and farmers. Cleared of tree stumps and brush, the soil produced large crops of hay, wheat, and grain. Fruit trees, including apple, cherry, peach, and pear thrived, and many Grand Island farmers raised chickens and cattle.

Lewis Allen bought six hundred acres on the south side of the island. He later gave two acres of this farm to his son, William Cleveland Allen, who built a villa there called *River Lea*. New York State almost demolished the house in the 1960s, after buying the property to enlarge Beaver Island State Park. The Grand Island Historical Society convinced the state to restore the house instead, because Lewis Allen's most famous nephew—President Grover Cleveland—visited it several times.

Allen had gotten his eighteen-year-old nephew hired as a clerk by Bowen and Rogers, the Buffalo law firm that handled his business affairs, in 1855. Cleveland passed the New York bar in 1859, became assistant attorney general for Erie County in 1863, and was elected mayor of Buffalo in 1881. He won the New York governor's race in 1883 and then the presidency in 1884. Cleveland returned to the White House in 1893, the only president to serve two, nonconsecutive terms (he won the 1888 popular vote, but lost the Electoral vote to Benjamin Harrison).

Grand Island became a popular vacation spot in the late 1800s. Ferries with names such as *Silver Spray*, *Island Belle*, and *Huntress* brought wealthy visitors from Buffalo. Wooden hotels, piers, and fishing clubs dotted the riverfront. A resort called Sheenwater opened an amusement park in the 1890s, and the island's first bicycle path was paved with cinders in 1900.

The resorts faded after the turn of the century. There were no bridges to the island until 1935, and ferry service depended on the weather. Wealthy travelers began driving their automobiles to newer—and easier to reach—lakeshore resorts. Some of the old wooden hotels burned, others were demolished.

Grand Island residents and businessmen had been campaigning for a bridge since the 1850s, when their town separated from the mainland city of Tonawanda. Congress debated building a bridge in the 1890s, and the islanders later petitioned the state of New York. The New York Central and the American Niagara Railroad Corporation considered building bridges in the 1920s.

Governor Franklin Roosevelt signed the Niagara Frontier Bridge Commission into existence in 1929. Four years later, Robert Moses tapped the federal government's new Reconstruction Finance Corporation for funding. Congress had chartered the RFC in 1932, to provide loans to state and local governments; though suggested by outgoing president Herbert Hoover, it became an important part of Roosevelt's "New Deal." Robert Moses, appointed chairman of the State of New York's Council of Parks in 1924, had created Jones Beach and laid out Long Island's highways.

With the federal loan, two bridges were built: one at the north end of the island, one at the south. Construction began in October 1933, and both spans were completed in less than two years. On opening day—July 13, 1935—an automobile parade crossed the South Grand Island Bridge to Tonawanda, drove north into Niagara Falls, and then returned over the North Grand Island Bridge.

The New York Thruway was begun in 1954. The section now known as I-190, which connects Buffalo and Lewiston, crossed Grand Island in 1958. Soon the old bridges, built to carry one lane in each direction, were overwhelmed. In 1963, the Thruway Authority built a duplicate of the South Grand Island Bridge alongside the original; the 1935 bridge carries southbound traffic, the 1963 span northbound. A duplicate of the North Grand Island Bridge opened in 1965.

In the 1950s, New York created two state parks on Grand Island. At the south end, Beaver Island has sand beaches, the restored River Lea Villa, an eighteen-hole golf course, a marina, and a nature center. Buckhorn Island, in the north, is an 895-acre nature preserve, with hiking trails through the Niagara River wetlands.

The 1950s and 1960s were also the years when the Army built about 250 Nike missile bases to defend major cities and industrial targets against Russian bombers. Western New York had seven Nike bases, each consisting of a control center and a launch site, where the guided missiles were stored underground. By the 1970s, when intercontinental missiles replaced bombers, the entire system was obsolete. The missiles were removed, the bases closed. Many were given to local governments.

Grand Island's control center is now Nike Base Park, with sports fields, a senior citizens' residence, and town maintenance buildings. The local school board transformed the nearby launch site into the Eco Island Ecology Reserve, with a pond, a butterfly garden, and classrooms in the old barracks.

The **South Grand Island Bridges** photographed from East River Road on Grand Island.

Did you know?

Where Grand Island divides the Niagara River, the western (or Canadian) branch is called the Chippewa Channel, the eastern the Tonawanda Channel. The Chippewa, or *Ojibwa*, were one of North America's largest Indian nations. Though the meaning of the Iroquois name *Tonawanda* has eluded historians, the Niagara Peninsula includes a City and a Town of Tonawanda, as well as a North Tonawanda. When the Erie Canal opened in 1825, water for the western section was drawn from Tonawanda Creek, which empties into the Niagara.

The **North Grand Island Bridges**, photographed from Niagara Falls, New York. The riverfront walking path is part of the Niagara Falls Greenway, a system of connected parks following the New York shoreline from Buffalo to Lake Ontario.

Chapter Five
Navy Island

AN INTERNATIONAL BOUNDARY COMMISSION decided in 1822 that the New York / Ontario border should follow the Niagara's deepest channel. Because this channel lay west of Grand Island, the smaller island northwest of Grand became part of Canada.

The Native Americans who fished around this island called it "Big Canoe." To the French it was *Île de la Marina*, where they built four flat-bottomed *batteaux* to ferry supplies to their Great Lakes trading posts. The British, who seized control of the Niagara in 1763, translated the French name as "Navy Island" and built a small shipyard, which they abandoned after launching a handful of schooners and sloops.

William Lyon MacKenzie, born in Scotland, moved to Canada in 1820. He established his first newspaper, *The Colonial Advocate*, four years later, and was elected to the Parliament of Upper Canada in 1829. After visiting the United States and meeting President Andrew Jackson, he returned home convinced that Canada should also be free of British rule. To spread the word, he started a second newspaper, *The*

Constitution, in which he reprinted Thomas Paine's revolutionary *Common Sense*.

MacKenzie wrote a Declaration of Independence on December 1, 1837, announcing the separation of the Republic of Canada from the British Empire. As the Republic's leader, he enlisted the support of wealthy Americans and landed hundreds of volunteers on Navy Island to invade Ontario. Each afternoon, the American steamship *Caroline* delivered food, money, and guns. By December 29, MacKenzie had a thousand men on the island.

Late that night, five boatloads of British troops boarded the *Caroline* at her dock. They chased the crew ashore, set the ship on fire, and turned her loose in the Niagara; she was still burning when she slid over the falls. President Martin Van Buren protested this attack on American citizens and property, but the British government claimed it had acted in self-defense; politicians and lawyers still refer to this "*Caroline* Affair" when discussing "preemptive strikes."

MacKenzie was arrested in Buffalo, charged with violating America's neutrality, and sentenced to eighteen months in prison. Without leadership or supplies, his supporters quickly abandoned Navy Island. After serving less than one year of his sentence, MacKenzie moved to New York City, where he supported himself for the next decade as an editor, writer, and newspaper publisher. He returned to Canada in 1850 and won a seat in Parliament the following year.

Navy Island, a mile long and half a mile wide, attracted little attention for the next hundred years. A few families farming there in the 1850s, and the two-story Queens Hotel opened in 1875. It closed early in the twentieth century, like the Grand Island resorts, and burned in 1910.

In 1945, American and Canadian businessmen recommended building the United Nations headquarters on Navy Island—the perfect location, they said, because it sat on the border between two nations that had been at peace for more than a century. An artist's watercolor sketch shows the tiny island covered with futuristic buildings and monuments, with bridges to Grand Island and Ontario; in the background, clouds of mist hang over Niagara Falls. Their bid was rejected, and the UN buildings were completed in 1952, on seventeen acres along New York's East River, which John D. Rockefeller, Jr. had purchased and then donated to the city.

Canada's Niagara Parks Commission began leasing Navy Island in 1938. Declared a Wildlife and Game Preserve in 1949, it is completely undeveloped and accessible only by boat. Deer live in the thick forest, and the shores are popular with fishermen and birdwatchers.

Chapter Six
The Falls and the Gorge

THE NIAGARA RIVER runs west from Grand Island to the falls, so that for a few miles, the Canadian shore is south of New York. Half a mile from the brink, the river divides around Goat Island. Ten percent of its water tumbles over the American Falls, onto mounds of rock a hundred feet high. The rest pours over the Horseshoe Fall on the Canadian side.

Father Louis Hennepin, chaplain to the French fur trader and explorer René Robert Cavalier, wrote the first eyewitness description of the falls in 1678:

> Betwixt the Lake Ontario and Erie is a vast and prodigious Cadence of Water which falls down after a surprising and astonishing manner, insomuch that the Universe does not afford its Parallel ... making an outrageous Noise, more terrible than that of thunder ...

The **American Falls** and **Goat Island** photographed from Prospect Point in New York's Niagara Falls State Park. The mist in the background hides the larger Horseshoe Fall.

Unfortunately, Hennepin was prone to exaggeration. He described the falls as being six or eight hundred feet high, said they could be heard from forty-five miles away, and later described travels and discoveries which historians have dismissed as wild imaginings.

As a young man, René Robert Cavalier joined the Jesuit Order. The vow of poverty he took prevented him from inheriting his parents' estate, La Salle, even after he left the Order. He moved to Canada—then known as New France—in 1667, and King Louis XIV granted him a fur trading concession and the title Sieur de La Salle *in 1675. Determined to make his fortune in the New World, La Salle explored the Ohio and*

Mississippi Rivers and claimed all of "Louisiana" for France. In 1678, he led an expedition up the Niagara River from Lake Ontario, past the rapids and falls. Where the river became navigable again, he built and launched Le Griffon, *the first sailing ship to cross Lake Erie (there is a Griffon Park on the New York side of the river, commemorating the occasion). It was during this expedition that Father Hennepin first saw the falls.*

TWELVE THOUSAND YEARS AGO, melting Ice Age glaciers filled ancient basins and rifts to form the five Great Lakes and the Saint Lawrence River. By seven thousand years ago, changes in the landscape had diverted all the water flowing north from Lake Erie into the Niagara River.

The falls were born seven miles north of their present location, where the river spilled over the Niagara Escarpment, a thousand-mile line of cliffs stretching east to west across New York State and southern Ontario. The rushing water wore away the face of the cliff, revealing layers of soft shale below the limestone riverbed. Spray from the waterfall then eroded the shale, excavating a cavern under the riverbed; when the bed collapsed, new layers of shale were exposed to the spray, and the process began all over again.

Over thousands of years, the river has carved a narrow gorge seven miles long and more than three hundred feet deep at its northern end. The widest part—twelve hundred feet across—is in front of the falls. Two miles north, the average width drops to 750 feet, and in one spot, the river is only 250 feet wide.

The **Niagara Gorge Discovery Center,** in Niagara Falls, New York, has exhibits on the history and the formation of the gorge. Summertime visitors can take guided tours of the rim and gorge trails, starting from the nearby Trailhead Center.

Though not as well-known as the falls, the Niagara Gorge offers some of the area's most impressive scenery. Visitors to Canada can ride an elevator down to the White Water Walk, a thousand-foot boardwalk overlooking the rapids, or descend a stairway to the riverbank at Niagara Glen. On the American side, stone stairways wind down to the river from overlooks at Whirlpool and Devil's Hole State Parks. Fishing is popular along both banks.

The Niagara is still cutting this gorge, most noticeably at the center of the Horseshoe. The first known picture of the falls, published in the 1697 edition of Father Hennepin's *A New*

Discovery of a Vast Country in America, shows the crest south of Goat Island as a straight line. By the late 1700s, the line had begun curving inward, taking a "horseshoe" shape.

British geologist Sir Charles Lyell visited Niagara Falls in 1841 with James Hall, one of the directors of the New York State Geological Survey. Unable to measure the rate of recession, Lyell guessed that it was less than one foot every year. Based on the length of the gorge, he then estimated that the falls were thirty-five thousand years old. (In his three-volume *Principles of Geology*, Lyell challenged the prevailing theory of "Catastrophism," which described the world as a young place rapidly shaped by cataclysmic floods and quakes. By arguing for a much older Earth, gradually shaped by measurable processes, Lyell helped shape the thoughts and writings of Charles Darwin.)

When Hall returned to Niagara Falls in 1842, he installed stone markers to help surveyors record changes in the shape of the crest. For an 1886 report to the United States Geological Survey, Robert Simpson Woodward—an astronomer, mathematician, and physicist—used these markers to estimate that the center of the Horseshoe was receding five feet every year. From Lyell's thirty-five thousand years, Woodward whittled the age of the falls down to seven thousand years.

Though modern geologists have reached a similar conclusion, they reject the nineteenth-century assumption that the recession occurred at a steady rate. Instead, they see the river working quickly at some times, slowly at others, depending on the annual flow and the hardness of the underlying rock.

The three–hundred-foot stairway at **Devil's Hole State Park** has more than four hundred steps.

Did you know?

Father Louis Hennepin arrived in Quebec as a Franciscan missionary in 1675. There is a Hennepin Road named after him on Grand Island, and a Hennepin Park in both Buffalo and Niagara Falls, New York. Because he also wrote the first description of Saint Anthony Falls, the only waterfall on the Mississippi River, there is also a Father Louis Hennepin Bridge and a Hennepin Island in Minneapolis.

Like its neighbor at Devil's Hole State Park, the stone stairway at **Whirlpool State Park** was built in the 1920s and is showing its age.

The **Great Gorge Railway** opened in 1895. In 1902, it was combined with the Niagara Falls Park & River Railway on the Canadian rim, creating a twenty-mile scenic loop that crossed the river on the Upper Steel Arch Bridge and the Queenston-Lewiston Suspension Bridge. Summertime trolleys had open sides for sightseeing, and starting in 1914, spotlights illuminated the upper rapids for nighttime travelers. Today, all that remains is the crumbling roadbed on the American side. The Canadian line went out of business in 1932, and the Great Gorge was shut down three years later, after a rockslide destroyed two hundred feet of track north of the Whirlpool Rapids Bridge.

Left: A modern view of the giant rock, a popular landmark along the Great Gorge route.

Morning sunlight reflects from the **American Rapids,** between the New York shore and Goat Island in Niagara Falls State Park.

Chapter Seven
Goat Island

In 1779, landowner John Stedman left his herd of goats on the island which separated the American from the Horseshoe Falls. He correctly assumed the rapids would protect the animals from the bears and wolves that hunted the mainland but did not count on an unusually harsh winter. Finding only one survivor in the spring—the rest of the herd had frozen to death—Stedman called the half-mile spit of land "the Goat's Island."

FOR HUNDREDS OF YEARS, Native Americans had carried—or "portaged"—their trade goods and bark canoes around the rapids and falls. Beginning at Lower Landing—present-day Lewiston—they climbed the steep Niagara Escarpment, and then followed the east rim of the gorge south to the falls. The trail ended above the American rapids, where the river again became navigable (today, the spot is marked by the New York Power Authority's twin intake towers).

The Iroquois Confederacy shared this trail with the French, who traded generously with local tribes and employed hundreds of Seneca men to carry goods up the escarpment. Control shifted to the British after 1759, when Sir William Johnson captured Fort Niagara, where the Niagara met Lake

Ontario. Appointed Superintendent of Indian Affairs because of his long friendship with the natives—he spoke the Mohawk language and had eight children by his common-law Indian wife—Johnson tried to make the transition peaceful.

John Stedman, who was appointed "Master of the Niagara Portage" in 1762, cared more about profits. He had the portage road rebuilt so oxen could haul wagons over the escarpment, eliminating hundreds of Seneca jobs. He also traded as little as possible with the natives and denied them access to "his" land along the river.

Many of the Great Lakes tribes challenged British rule after the French and Indian War, in what became known as "Pontiac's Rebellion." Pontiac was an Ottawa war chief, who tried—unsuccessfully—to capture Fort Detroit in May 1763. Over the next few years, several smaller British forts fell to native attacks, and both sides committed atrocities. When peace was arranged in 1766, neither side could claim victory; the Native Americans never accepted British authority, and the British continued clearing and settling land they felt they had "won" from the French.

On the morning of September 14, 1763, Stedman was leading a wagon train back to Lower Landing from Fort Schlosser, the British post above the falls. At Devil's Hole, where the Seneca believed an evil spirit haunted a cave, three hundred native warriors attacked with muskets, knives, and tomahawks.

Stedman turned his horse and ran home to Fort Schlosser; he would later claim he left the battle to warn the troops there.

The cliff at **Devil's Hole State Park**, photographed from the stairway. After the battle, the small stream that used to spill into the gorge here was named "Bloody Run."

Unfortunately, nobody warned the foot soldiers stationed at Lower Landing. Hearing gunfire, eighty-one of them charged up the escarpment into an ambush. To escape the carnage, drummer boy William Matthews jumped from the cliff; he survived only because his drum strap snagged in a tree.

All the others were killed.

Sir William Johnson arranged a peace treaty at Fort Niagara in 1764. For the rest of his life, Stedman claimed that at this meeting, the Seneca gave him title to all the land between Devil's Hole and Fort Schlosser, including the islands above the falls (by some accounts, Stedman also claimed to own the falls themselves). He planted the area's first orchards; ran a store, a tavern, and a sawmill; and returned to England a wealthy man in 1795.

The New York Legislature dismissed Stedman's property claims in 1801. Though he died seven years later, his heirs continued fighting for "their" lands until 1823.

BROTHERS AUGUSTUS AND PETER PORTER leased the Niagara Portage for their shipping company in 1803. Two years later, they bought a large piece of land along the Niagara River, where they built a grist mill and a tannery (leather factory). They also tried to buy Goat Island for a sheep pasture in 1811 but were told New York wanted the property for an armory, or maybe a prison.

Augustus Porter had been a surveyor for the Holland Land Company and was Niagara County's first judge and postmaster. His brother Peter had a law degree from Yale, won terms in the New York State Assembly and the United States Congress, and was a member of the Erie Canal Commission from 1810 until 1816. When the War of 1812 erupted, Peter Porter resigned from Congress, joined the Army, and fought in several major battles along the Niagara.

The Porters finally acquired Goat Island in November 1816 (the New York Legislature had voted to build the prison in Auburn). In the spring, they built a wooden toll bridge across the rapids, from the American shore to the east end of the island. This proved so popular that, in the words of Niagara historian Peter A. Porter (Augustus's grandson), "by the end of the year 1817 it was evident that Goat Island was worth more as a pleasure resort than it ever could be worth as a sheep pasture."

The stone bridge from Niagara Falls, New York to Green Island (formerly Bath Island) is one of a pair of 1901 spans known as the **American Falls Historic Bridges**; the other crosses the rapids from Green Island to Goat Island. Though these bridges are among the most recognizable structures in Niagara Falls State Park, rushing water and harsh winters have taken their toll. To maintain safe access to the islands, the state built temporary steel pedestrian bridges across both spans in 2004.

Winter ice swept the bridge away in 1818. To replace it, the Porters built two sturdier wooden bridges closer to the falls, where the ice was usually too fragmented to do much damage. The first crossed from the American shore to Bath Island, where the brothers would later build a paper mill; the second connected Bath to Goat Island.

The New York Power Authority and the Bethlehem Steel Company built the **American Rapids Bridge** in 1959, to provide automobile access to Goat Island. This picture was taken from the north shore of Goat Island, looking toward the falls, with one of the American Falls Historic Bridges in the background.

Peter A. Porter explained how the bridges were built, one section at a time, in his 1900 book *Goat Island*:

> ...two logs, parallel and some 8 feet apart, were laid on rollers, and with their shore ends heavily weighted with stone, were pushed out over the rapids. On each log a man walked out to the end, carrying with him a sharp iron pointed staff.

The staffs were driven into the riverbed and lashed to the logs, anchoring them in place. Planks laid across the logs formed a roadway, over which workers dragged heavy stones to build a pier in the rapids, underneath the ends of the logs. When this first pier was completed, two more logs were rolled out from it, and so on until the bridge reached the opposite shore. These bridges remained in use until 1855, when they were rebuilt of iron. But according to Porter, not everyone was impressed:

> Red Jacket, the famous Seneca, was on the bank an interested spectator. As the first span was successfully completed ... someone asked him what he thought of it. Rising majestically and drawing his blanket close about him, he muttered: "Damn Yankee," and stalked away.

The Porters later built a chain of bridges connecting three small islands in the Canadian Rapids, south of Goat Island. In 1816, when ice jams filled the streams between them, hotel owner Parkhurst Whitney had walked out to the islands with his daughters Asenath, Angeline, and Celinda Eliza. Augustus Porter agreed to name the islands after the girls, and they are still known as the Three Sisters; a smaller island, not accessible by bridge, is called Solon (or Little Brother) after Whitney's son.

Author H.G. Wells set part of his 1907 science fiction novel *War in the Air* on Goat Island; bicycle repairman Bert Smallways is stranded there while fleets of airships battle overhead for control of the hydroelectric plants surrounding the falls. Wells had visited Niagara the year before while touring the eastern United States and writing a series of articles for Harper's Magazine (later published as *The Future in America: A Search After Realities.*) He said that his favorite view was not of the falls, "but to look up-stream from Goat Island and see the sea-wide crest of the flashing sunlit rapids against the gray-blue sky. That was like a limitless ocean pouring down a sloping world towards one…"

Did you know?

Travelers of the late 1700s called our American Falls the "Fort Schlosser Fall." The British built the fort—named for its first commander, Captain Joseph Schlosser—in 1760, on the site of "Little Fort Niagara," which the French had abandoned in 1759. The British gave Fort Schlosser to the United States in 1796, and then recaptured and burned it during the War of 1812. All that remains is a thirty-foot stone chimney, built in 1750 for the French fort. Several houses, including John Stedman's, were built around the chimney before the Niagara Falls Power Company bought the riverfront property in 1890. The chimney has been moved twice, in 1902 and 1942; both times, the stones were carefully marked and reassembled. Though surrounded by trees, it can still be seen from the Robert Moses State Parkway; local historians have suggested moving it again, closer to the tourist district.

The Porters tried to rename Goat Island "Iris Island," after the rainbows that formed in the mist, but most visitors and guidebooks continued using the older name.

The **American Falls**, as seen from Niagara Falls, Canada. The main cascade, 830 feet wide, is separated from the narrow Bridal Veil by Luna Island. Below the falls are mounds of fallen rock called talus slopes, which are between 80 and 110 feet high. The land to the left of the falls is Prospect Park, and to the right is part of Goat Island, which separates the American Falls from the Canadian Horseshoe.

Page 48: Three elevators carry visitors to the observation deck and revolving restaurant atop Canada's 520-foot **Skylon** Tower, which was completed in October 1965.

Chapter Eight
Clifton, Elgin, and Niagara Falls

WHEN BRITISH TRAVEL WRITER and illustrator John Maude visited Niagara Falls in 1800, it took him two months to get there from New York City. Five years later, Massachusetts Speaker of the House Timothy Bigelow made the round trip from Boston in six weeks but did not find the going any easier. Maude described one New York road as "tolerable for two or three miles, then execrable," and Bigelow remembered crossing "a new wooden bridge over the Mohawk" that was "already ruinous … we thought it not impossible that it might fall while we were on it." The accommodations were even worse. One tavern, Maude complained, "is a house in which filth and famine strive for mastery;" at another, Bigelow was "told that our sheets were clean, for they had been slept in but five times since they were washed."

Despite these problems, the falls drew enough travelers in the early 1800s to support little resorts on both sides of the river. Charles Wilson built a tavern on the Canadian side, overlooking the Horseshoe, in 1797. Twenty years later, when his widow sold the property to William Forsyth, summer visitors had their choice of small hotels.

William Forsyth was born in northeastern New York but came to Ontario with his family when he was twelve years old. He joined the militia for the War of 1812 but may also have been a smuggler and a war profiteer. After the war, the Ontario government denied him the small fortune he demanded for repairing his home and farm, which had been damaged by American soldiers; he later settled for a smaller sum.

Forsyth renamed Wilson's Tavern "The Niagara Falls Hotel," and then built a covered stairway down to Table Rock, the best spot for viewing both the American and the Horseshoe falls. (A broad overhang exposed by the falls' recession, Table Rock no longer exists. Pieces began falling into the gorge as early as 1818, and a third of the Rock broke away in 1850. The Canadian government blasted the rest in 1935, to prevent it falling on the Ontario Power Company's hydroelectric plant.)

By 1820, Forsyth was running stagecoaches from Buffalo, Fort Erie, and Newark (now Niagara-on-the-Lake). He also had competition: John Brown, who built the Ontario House and started his own stagecoach. Forsyth fought back in 1822, demolishing Wilson's tavern and replacing it with the three-story Pavilion Hotel, then the largest building on either side of the falls. Four years later, Brown's Ontario House burned, and Forsyth added two large bedroom wings to the Pavilion (Forsyth's enemies claimed the two events were related).

In 1786, the British had established a military reserve along the Canadian riverbank and gorge. Because this property was one "chain" wide—a standard measurement, equal to sixty-six feet—it was called the Chain Reserve. Forsyth asked to lease part of it in 1820 but was turned down. In 1827, he did not ask—just fenced the section he wanted, blocking the road John Brown's guests used to visit Table Rock. The government removed the fences twice, and then in 1832, forced Forsyth to sell his hotel and other properties. The new City of the Falls Company bought four hundred acres to build a residential community but went out of business after selling only a handful of lots. The Pavilion burned in 1839, was rebuilt on a smaller scale four years later, and burned again in 1865.

Ogden Creighton, a retired British Army Captain, bought the hillside facing the American Falls in 1830. He named the area Clifton, laid out streets and building lots, and built a home he called Clifton Cottage. Like the City of the Falls Company, he failed to sell many lots, and left Clifton with his family in the 1840s.

Ontario businessman Samuel Zimmerman bought Creighton's property for a private estate. He had four massive gatehouses built, one at each corner, but saw only the foundation of the mansion completed before dying in an 1857 railroad disaster.

Zimmerman had made his fortune building parts of the Great Western Railroad and the Welland Canal, which allowed ships to bypass the Niagara River. He also invested heavily in the first suspension bridge over the Niagara Gorge, and when it opened in 1848, founded the Village of Elgin on the Canadian side. Named for the Canadian Governor, Lord Elgin, the village soon boasted half a dozen hotels, including the Elgin House and the Suspension Bridge Hotel. The Town of Clifton absorbed Elgin in 1856, and then changed its name to Niagara Falls in 1881.

Postcard view of the second **Clifton House Hotel**. Harmanus Crysler built the first Clifton House in the early 1830s. Three stories high, with sixty bedrooms, it was still one of the town's most popular hotels in 1898, when it was consumed by a fire that started in the boiler house chimney. The five-story building in the picture was built in 1905 and had 270 rooms. Destroyed by a fire on December 31, 1932, it was never rebuilt; since 1937, the property has been occupied by the Oakes Garden Theatre, an outdoor amphitheater overlooking the American Falls.

John T. Bush, who owned the International Hotel in Niagara Falls, New York, built his Clifton Place mansion on Zimmerman's foundation in the 1860s. His family lived there until 1927, when millionaire Harry Oakes bought the property.

The American Falls, framed by decorative columns, provide a backdrop for the raised bandstand at **Oakes Garden Theatre**.

Born in Sangerville, Maine in 1874, Harry Oakes quit medical school in the late 1890s to search for gold, first in Alaska, then in California and Australia. His efforts paid off in 1912, when he discovered both an iron mine and North America's second-largest gold mine near the shores of Ontario's Kirkland Lake. After moving to Niagara Falls in 1924, he restored the old Portage Road and donated a twenty-acre park and athletic field to the city. When the second Clifton House hotel burned in 1932, he bought the property and gave it to the Niagara Parks Commission; five years later, he had the Clifton Place estate razed, leaving just the antique fountain in Queen Victoria Park.

Surrounded by the colorful restaurants, shops, and museums of the Clifton Hill Tourist District, the 175-foot **Niagara Sky Wheel** opened on June 17, 2005. Each of the 42 heated and air-conditioned cars carries eight passengers.

In 1943, Harry Oakes was murdered at his home in the Bahamas, where he had been living since 1934, when the Canadian government raised his income tax rate to eighty-five percent; his killer was never found. Several places in Niagara Falls, Ontario, are named after him, including Oakes Park, the Oakes Garden Theatre, and the twenty-one story Oakes Hotel.

The area above the Horseshoe Fall has been called "Fallsview" since the 1880s, when Michigan Central and Canadian Southern trains stopped there to give passengers a look at the falls. On June 10, 2004, the Ontario government opened the billion-dollar **Niagara Fallsview Casino** complex (left), which includes a thirty-story hotel. Part of the casino was designed around the façade of the Ontario Power Company's 1904 distribution building (the hydroelectric plant, no longer in operation, sits on the riverbank below the tourist district).

The 325-foot **Konica Minolta Tower** *(right)*, built in 1962 as the Seagram Tower, now houses the Tower Hotel and the Pinnacle Restaurant. Walt Disney visited the tower in 1963, and briefly considered building an attraction there modeled after Disneyland's popular "Rocket to the Moon" ride.

The **Casino Niagara**, which opened in December 1996, occupies a former shopping mall called Maple Leaf Village. The 355-foot steel tower was built in 1964 by Oneida Community, Ltd., which had been manufacturing silverware in Niagara Falls since 1917 (the company was formed in western New York in 1879, after the Oneida religious commune dissolved). The tower originally had two observation decks, topped by a fifty-foot neon sign. The sign was removed in 1974, and during the Maple Leaf Village years, the tower bore Kodak's name. It is not currently open to visitors.

Postcard view of the **Cataract House Hotel**.

PARKHURST WHITNEY WAS FIVE YEARS OLD in 1789, the year his family moved from Massachusetts to Ontario County, New York. He bought a farm four miles above Niagara Falls in 1810 and joined the militia in 1812. After the war, he leased the Eagle Tavern, one of the only buildings left standing when the British burned the Village of Niagara Falls. In 1818, he teamed up with William Forsyth to launch the first ferry below the falls. Forsyth built a wooden stairway on the Canadian side, Whitney on the American; rowboats carried passengers between the landings.

In the early 1830s, Whitney bought the Cataract House, the three-story hotel that had opened across the street from his Eagle Tavern in 1825. Whitney added wings and porches, even a ballroom that extended over the American rapids, making the Cataract House the largest and most popular hotel on the American side; a young Abraham Lincoln signed the guest register in 1853.

Postcard view of the **International Hotel**.

Though it changed hands several times, the Cataract House remained a Niagara Falls landmark until October 1945, when it was destroyed by fire.

By 1892, there were more than forty hotels in Niagara Falls, New York, including the Kaltenback, the Prospect, the Imperial, the United States, and the Temperance House. One of the biggest was the International Hotel, built on the corner of Falls and Main Streets in 1853. "Only Hotel With Passenger Elevator," boasted an 1876 advertisement, which also showed new wings built over the American Rapids (these were demolished, along with the Cataract House's ballroom, after the Niagara Reservation was established in 1885). Fire claimed the International in 1918.

Most unusual may have been the Tower Hotel, near Prospect Point. The tower that rose above it was 250 feet high, with three observation decks, elevators, and a stairway. Though one of Niagara's most popular landmarks—it appears in many old photographs and postcard views—the owners removed the tower in 1904, after a neighbor sued over ice falling from the upper levels onto his museum's roof. The De Forrest Wireless Telegraph Company reassembled it in St. Louis as the "Tower of Wireless Telegraphy" for that summer's Louisiana Purchase Exposition, and inventor Guglielmo Marconi sent one of the world's first wireless messages from the top. Two years later, the tower was moved to its final home: Hot Springs Mountain, Arkansas, where it stood as a tourist attraction until 1975, when it was declared unsafe and demolished.

Did you know?

A few hours before President William McKinley was assassinated in Buffalo, he and his wife visited the International Hotel for lunch.

In March 1848, ice jams in the Niagara River stopped water flowing over the falls for most of a day. Though the falls themselves do not freeze, ice often piles up in the river below them. Visitors were allowed to walk across these "ice bridges" until 1912, when a collapse killed three people.

Chapter Nine

The Maid of the Mist

THE FIRST *MAID OF THE MIST* was a side wheel steamboat, launched on May 27, 1846 as a passenger ferry (all the earlier ferries, since 1818, had been rowboats). Two years later, business dropped off when the first suspension bridge opened. To make up for lost revenue, the *Maid*'s captain began taking sightseers for close-up views of the falls. This worked out so well that in 1854, her owners launched a larger paddle-wheel steamer, the *Maid of the Mist II*, built especially for the sightseeing trade.

After a few good years, business dwindled again. In 1861, a Montreal company bought the *Maid of the Mist II* at auction, with plans to run her as a ferry on the Saint Lawrence River. To complete the sale, the original owners agreed to deliver the boat from her Niagara Falls dock to Queenston, Ontario.

In between was a stretch of river many believed impassable.

The **Upper Whirlpool Rapids** photographed from the rim of the gorge in Whirlpool State Park.

Long before the Great Lakes formed, a river that geologists call the Saint David carved its own path across the Niagara Peninsula. This gorge stretched east to west, and when glaciers covered northern New York, they filled it in with loose rocks and gravel.

The slow, southward recession of Niagara Falls collided with Saint David's Buried Gorge a little more than four thousand years ago. The surging river quickly washed out all the loose rock in its path, carving a rounded basin seventeen hundred feet long and twelve hundred feet wide.

The **Niagara Whirlpool** photographed from the American shore in Whirlpool State Park.

The Niagara roars into this basin at speeds approaching forty miles an hour. Briefly diverted from its northerly course, the water sweeps counterclockwise around the rim, feeding a treacherous Whirlpool, 125 feet deep. For a mile above this Whirlpool, and another mile below, the river is shredded by some of the world's most dangerous rapids. North of the Whirlpool, the river plunges sixteen feet at Devil's Hole; overall, the river drops ninety feet in little more than two miles.

The rapids above the Whirlpool, photographed from the American shore in **Whirlpool State Park**. The waves were even higher in Robinson's time, before half of the Niagara's water was diverted to the hydroelectric plants at Lewiston and Queenston.

Joel Robinson, the *Maid*'s fifty-three-year-old captain, was offered five hundred dollars—more than thirteen thousand in modern currency—for the seven-mile voyage. Needing the money, and sure of himself and his vessel, he accepted the challenge. At three in the afternoon, June 6, 1861, he steamed north into the gorge. Thousands of spectators lined the riverbanks, but aboard the *Maid*, Robinson had only a mechanic, James McIntyre, and engineer James Jones.

As soon as she entered the rapids, the steamer became unmanageable. Some eyewitnesses said the waves breaking over her deck swept away her smokestack; others that the stack sheared off because it struck the suspension bridge's guy wires.

When the upper rapids hurled the *Maid* into the Whirlpool, fierce currents whipped her three times around the basin before Robison regained enough control to aim her into the lower rapids. Again, the waves broke over her deck, often hiding her from the spectators ashore. But seventeen minutes after leaving Niagara Falls, Captain Robinson delivered the *Maid of the Mist II* to the Queenston docks, more or less intact.

That evening, Joel Robinson told his wife he was retiring from steamboat piloting. He never returned to the river, and he died two years later.

Two new *Maid of the Mist* sightseeing steamers were launched in 1885 and 1892, the first from the Canadian shore, the second from the American. Both remained in service until April 1955, when they were destroyed by fire. As a temporary replacement, a forty-foot yacht nicknamed *Little Maid of the Mist* was towed down the service road to the Canadian shore a few weeks later. A third *Maid of the Mist I* launched from the Canadian shore that July; the following June, a new *Maid of the Mist II* was completed in New York. Both were built of steel, sixty-six feet long with two-hundred horsepower diesel engines and room for a hundred passengers. The most recent boat in the fleet, *Maid of the Mist VII*, was delivered in pieces by flatbed trailers, assembled on the Canadian shore, and launched on May 30, 1997. Driven by dual 350-horsepower engines, she carries six hundred people.

Maid of the Mist approaching the Horseshoe Fall, photographed from Niagara Falls State Park. The rocks in the foreground are part of Goat Island.

Every October, The *Maid of the Mist* fleet is removed from the river; so much water is diverted for electrical generation between November and April that the ships would founder at their docks. Until 2013, the ships were stored and repaired on the Canadian shore. In October 2013, the fleet was moved to new dry docks on the American shore, north of Prospect Park and the Rainbow Bridge.

Beginning in 2014, the Maid of the Mist *will operate only from the American shore. Visitors to the Canadian side will see the falls from a pair of seven-hundred passenger catamarans operated by Hornblower Niagara Cruises.*

THERE ARE SEVERAL VERSIONS of the Native American legend the first *Maid of the Mist* was named for. All involve a young native woman, Lelawala, and the Thunder God Heno, who was said to live in or behind the waterfall. Some tell that Lelawala rowed a canoe into the rapids and over the falls because she was overcome with grief after her husband died; others that she was fleeing an arranged marriage to a man she didn't love. In either case, she was saved by the Thunder God to live on as the "Maid of the Mist." In some versions Lelawala marries Heno; in others he sends her back to her village with warnings or wisdom. When a giant river serpent threatened her people, Heno killed it with a thunderbolt; the curve of its body wedged between the shores shaped the Horseshoe.

Unfortunately, the least accurate version of the story— based on La Salle's account of his travels—was the one told to generations of sightseers. Like many explorers and settlers, La Salle depicted the natives as ignorant savages, and claimed to have seen Lelawala sent over the falls as a *sacrifice* to the Thunder God. *Maid of the Mist* tour guides finally stopped telling this story after modern Iroquois (or *Haudenosaunee*, "People of the Long House") threatened to protest.

New York artist James Francis Brown (1862-1935) decorated the lobby of the Cataract House Hotel with two paintings inspired by the legend. "The Red Man's Fact" showed a stoic Lelawala paddling her white canoe over the falls, while "The White Man's Fancy" depicted the Maid of the Mist as a nude fairy dancing in the spray.

Did you know?

For those who want to experience the gorge rapids as Joel Robinson did aboard the *Maid of the Mist*, Jet Boat tours leave from both shores and plow south through the lower rapids into the Whirlpool. No boats dare the upper rapids, which are considered unnavigable.

Robinson Island is a tiny, wooded patch of land in the American Rapids. Some historians say that it was named after *Maid of the Mist* Captain Joel Robinson in 1838, when he rowed out to rescue a worker who had gotten stranded there after falling from the bridge to Goat Island. I prefer this story to the one Peter A. Porter told in his 1901 *Niagara Falls Guide Book*: that in 1860, Robinson walked across the rapids to the island, balancing himself with an iron staff… just to show that it could be done.

The Niagara River is 150 feet deep below the falls. The deep water absorbs the tremendous force of the cascade, leaving the surface calm enough for sightseeing boats, even within the curve of the Horseshoe.

Suspended from six, one-inch steel cables, the **Whirlpool Aero Car** carries sightseers across the Canadian side of the Whirlpool—250 feet above the water. Financed by Spanish investors and built in Bilbao, Spain in 1916, it was called the "Spanish Aero Car" until 2004. The Niagara Parks Commission has been operating the Aero Car since 1968.

Chapter Ten
The Rainbow Bridge

EVERY WINTER, ICE from Lake Erie tumbles over Niagara Falls. Jammed into the narrow gorge, this ice often forms a solid "ice bridge" stretching from shore to shore. In the winter of 1867-68, a rope was carried across this icepack, three hundred yards north of the American Falls. Secured to both sides of the gorge, it was used to guide wire cables across for the Falls View Suspension Bridge.

A bridge at this location was not a new idea. New York had granted a charter to the Niagara Falls Suspension Bridge Company in 1855, but no work was done until after the charter was renewed in April 1867. The Canadian Parliament gave a similar charter to the Clifton Suspension Bridge Company in May 1868, and the companies united that summer.

Samuel Keefer, who designed the span, had built Canada's first suspension bridge over the Ottawa River in 1844. He had also worked for the Erie and Welland Canals, built Canada's first railroad tunnel, and supervised the design and construction of the Parliament buildings in Ottawa.

Currier & Ives lithograph: a Canadian view of the first **Falls View Suspension Bridge**.

Four wooden towers, each one hundred feet tall, supported the cables which carried the roadway across the Niagara Gorge. The wooden deck was completed December 29, 1868 and opened the first Saturday in 1869.

The Falls View Suspension Bridge (or "Niagara-Clifton Bridge," as it was also known) was an immediate success, carrying thousands of wagons and pedestrians its first weekend. Keefer's design won a gold medal at the 1878 Paris *Exposition Universelle*, where visitors first saw the completed head of Frederic Bartholdi's *Liberty Enlightening the World*.

But the deck was only ten feet wide, which meant traffic could only move in one direction at a time. During the busy tourist months, long lines of wagons and cabs waited for the bell announcing it was their turn to cross.

In the 1880s, the Falls View was gradually rebuilt of steel. The towers were replaced in 1884, with an elevator on the Canadian side taking visitors to an observation deck. By the summer of 1888, all the wood had been removed and the deck had been widened to seventeen feet.

Heavy winds caused the bridge to sway. On the night of January 9, 1889, an American doctor crossed to tend a Canadian patient. When he returned to New York, shortly before midnight, he said the deck was rising and falling, twisting as much as forty-five degrees.

Twenty after three that morning, the bridge fell into the gorge and sank in the river.

The ruins were never recovered.

The Bridge Company's directors quickly ordered a replacement. Foundries worked around the clock forging new components from the same patterns they had used the year before. The steel parts were delivered seventy days after the collapse. Construction began on March 22, 1889 and was completed in thirty-eight days. On May 7, the second Falls View Suspension Bridge opened to traffic.

In January 1890, wind tried to claim this one, too. But although it was badly damaged, the bridge survived, and was quickly repaired... only to be declared obsolete a few years later, when electric trolleys replaced horse-drawn carriages.

To carry the trolleys, engineer Leffert L. Buck designed what was then the world's largest steel arch bridge. Completed in 1898, it had an 840-foot main span and carried two trolley tracks, two carriage lanes, and a pedestrian walk. Because it was upstream from Buck's 1897 arch bridge over the Whirlpool Rapids, it was called the Upper Steel Arch Bridge.

The Falls View Suspension Bridge was disassembled, and then rebuilt farther down the gorge.

Like the suspension bridges it replaced, the steel arch sometimes swayed in the wind. A year after it opened, the owners discovered an even greater threat. The arch was fourteen feet closer to the American Falls than the old suspension bridge, and the abutments were at the bottom of the gorge. In 1899, the ice plunging over Niagara Falls piled eighty feet high. To protect the bridge, engineers broke up the icepack with explosive.

On January 22, 1938, wind-driven ice filled the gorge again, destroying the American abutment. Five days later, the Canadian supports gave way and the bridge collapsed onto the ice. When the river thawed in April, the ruined span sank to the river bottom.

The Niagara Falls Bridge Commission met for the first time in August 1938. That November, they approved plans by Edward Lupfer and Richard Lee for a steel arch 950 feet across, spanning the gorge 550 feet north of the lost span. To prevent ice damage, they placed the abutments fifty feet above the riverbanks. King George VI and Queen Elizabeth dedicated the site on May 22, 1939, during their Royal Tour of Canada. Construction began the following spring, and the Rainbow Bridge opened November 1, 1941, carrying four lanes of traffic and a pedestrian walkway.

Formed to replace the Upper Steel Arch Bridge, the Niagara Falls Bridge Commission now operates all four international crossings: The Peace Bridge, the Rainbow Bridge, the Whirlpool Rapids Bridge, and the Lewiston-Queenston Bridge.

Looking south toward the **Rainbow Bridge**, from the walking trail on the American rim. In the background are the American Falls, the Prospect Point Observation Tower, and Goat Island.

Did you know?

The Upper Steel Arch Bridge was popularly known as the "Honeymoon Bridge." The tradition of honeymooning at the falls began in the early 1800s. Aaron Burr's daughter, Theodosia, visited with her husband in 1801, and Jerome Bonaparte—Napoleon's younger brother—brought his bride to the falls in 1804. "Every American bride is taken there," Oscar Wilde wrote in the 1880s. "The stupendous waterfall must certainly be one of the earliest, if not the keenest, disappointments in American married life."

The **Rainbow Bridge** photographed from Niagara Falls State Park.

Did you know?

The Royal Tour of 1939 was the first visit by a reigning British king to either Canada or the United States. King George VI and Queen Elizabeth crossed Canada by railroad; laid the cornerstone for the Supreme Court Building in Ottawa; toured the 1939 New York World's Fair; and visited President Franklin Roosevelt at his estate in Hyde Park, New York.

Top: The **Rainbow Tower Carillon,** overlooking the Canadian end of the Rainbow Bridge, was completed in 1947. The smallest of the fifty-nine tuned bells inside weighs nine pounds, the largest ten tons. Designed to be played with a keyboard and foot pedals, the instrument was automated in 2002, and now plays three times daily.

The Carillon is featured in the 1953 thriller *Niagara,* along with a chase on the spray-swept stairs of the Cave of the Winds and a helicopter rescue from the edge of the Horseshoe. Marilyn Monroe, in one of her first starring roles, plays Rose Loomis, who is plotting to have her husband killed. Early in the film, the Carillon's bells are seen in close-up, playing Rose's favorite song; later, they are silent witness to a murder. Watching *Niagara* after visiting the falls is like taking a trip back in time. On the American side, the Prospect Point Observation Tower hasn't been built yet. On the Canadian, the main characters are vacationing in rustic cabins within sight of the falls. Without high-rise hotels or casinos, the 165-foot Carillon is the tallest building on the cliff.

Bottom: In the early 1950s, the Boy Scouts of America donated about two hundred eight-foot replicas of the **Statue of Liberty** to cities and towns across the United States. This one stands in a small park on Rainbow Boulevard, near the American entrance to the Rainbow Bridge.

The **Great Falls** in Paterson, New Jersey, where Sam Patch became known as "the Jersey Jumper."

Chapter Eleven
The Daredevils

SAM PATCH BEGAN WORKING twelve-hour days when he was seven years old, spinning cotton in Pawtucket, Rhode Island. Like many of the local boys, he spent his Sundays swimming or fishing in the Blackstone River, below the fifty-foot fall that powered the mills.

The more daring boys—Sam among them—also enjoyed jumping from the top of the cliff into the deep pool at the foot of the falls. When a new, six-story mill opened in 1813, Sam began leaping from the roof, one hundred feet above the pool. He held his body rigid and hit feet first, taking a deep breath before impact. If the townspeople gathered to watch, he held his breath and remained underwater until they feared for his life.

By the 1820s, Patch was spinning cotton in Paterson, New Jersey, another mill town built around a waterfall: The Great Falls of the Passaic River. On September 30, 1827, most of the city turned out to watch mill owner Thomas Crane complete a wooden bridge over the waterfall.

Earlier that summer, Crane had bought the land north of the falls, where locals used to gather for informal picnics. He renamed the property Forest Garden, laid out gravel paths, and built an outdoor restaurant and ice cream parlor. Admission would be charged at the bridge.

Sam Patch interrupted Crane's ceremony by stepping off the edge of the cliff and dropping seventy feet into the foam below the falls. To identify himself with the city's workers, he wore the white cotton parade uniform of the Paterson Association of Spinners. When asked why he jumped, he said he wanted "to show that some things can be done as well as others." He repeated this statement so many times over the next two years that it became his trademark.

The following summer, Patch jumped the Great Falls on the Fourth of July, and then again on July 21. He advertised both stunts in advance, and on July 21, drew a crowd of between six and ten thousand—more than lived in the city. In August, he jumped at Hoboken, a hundred feet from a ship's mast into the Hudson River.

The now-famous "Jersey Jumper" came to Niagara Falls in October 1829. Hotel owners Forsyth, Whitney, and Brown had invited him to be part of an afternoon of spectacles, including a staged shipwreck and the detonation of explosives along the crest of the Horseshoe. Patch would jump from a wooden ladder on Goat Island.

The explosions were barely heard over the roar of the falls, and the ship set loose above the rapids foundered on a rock instead of tumbling over the edge. Patch rescheduled his jump for the following afternoon, because the workers setting up his ladder had damaged it.

When the advertised time arrived, a storm blew in. Patch and his audience waited it out, and then he climbed the ladder to a platform eighty feet above the river and jumped. As he had practiced at Pawtucket, he remained underwater until many of the spectators were sure he had drowned.

Patch scheduled his next Niagara jump for Saturday, October 17. He advertised by appearing nightly at Jonathan McCleary's Buffalo Museum, which housed paintings, Indian artifacts, and curiosities donated by local citizens. On the morning of the seventeenth, he rode a steam ship from Buffalo to Niagara Falls, where he thrilled the passengers by leaping from the mast into the river. By three o'clock, two thousand spectators had gathered around the falls. Patch walked down to a new platform, 120 feet above the water. He kissed the American flag waving there, then stepped off and disappeared into the spray. As always, he waited at least a minute before surfacing to cheers and applause.

Despite his growing fame, Patch was often described as "melancholy." He spent most of his time drinking, and many considered him suicidal. On November 6, he leapt one hundred feet into the Genesee Falls at Rochester, a fast-growing New York mill town on the Erie Canal. Disappointed with the size of the crowd, he announced that he would jump again one week later—on Friday the Thirteenth. He printed an elaborate handbill and built a higher platform, 125 feet above the water. On the thirteenth, ten or twelve thousand people lined the cliffs (Rochester's population was about nine thousand).

After what many remembered as a drunken speech, Sam Patch stepped off the platform and crashed into the water. His body was found in the spring, several miles downriver, and buried in a pauper's grave. Until the middle of the twentieth century, when local high school students raised money to buy him a headstone, his only marker was a wooden board reading:

Born in Livorno, Italy, **Maria Spelterini** began performing in her father's circus when she was three years old. In this picture (from an 1876 stereopticon card), she is crossing the Niagara Gorge on a tightrope north of Roebling's Suspension Bridge. For this crossing, she wore peach baskets on her feet to make the stunt more difficult. She would also cross the tightrope blindfolded, and once in shackles.

SAM PATCH
SUCH IS FAME

In the months after his final leap, rumors spread that Sam Patch had faked his death. He was the larger-than-life hero of poems and plays in the 1830s and 1840s, and of an illustrated children's book, *The Wonderful Leaps of Sam Patch*, in 1870. President Andrew Jackson owned a white horse named Sam Patch, on which he sat for a portrait by painter Ralph Earl.

JEAN-FRANÇOISE GRAVELET came to the United States in 1855 with the popular Ravel Troupe of French acrobats and equestrians. By the time the troupe played Niagara Falls in 1858, the golden-haired rope walker had adopted the stage name "Charles Blondin."

He returned to Niagara in June 1859. The authorities would not allow him to stretch his rope directly above the falls, from Goat Island to the Canadian shore. Some thought the stunt would be undignified; most believed it would end with his death.

When Blondin was four years old, a circus troupe played his hometown of Saint Omer, in northeastern France. At home after the show, he tried walking on a rope tied between two chairs. The chairs toppled, so he tried again with a rope stretched across a gateway; luckily, all he broke when he fell was the fishing pole he carried for balance. Impressed by the boy's persistence, his father—who had once been a gymnast—enrolled him in the *École de Gymnase* at Lyon. Six months later, young Jean-Françoise was performing in public. Newspaper writers called him "The Boy Wonder."

Blondin advertised his Niagara crossing for June 30, at five in the afternoon. His Manila hemp rope was thirteen hundred feet long, but only three inches in diameter. He tied one end to a tree in what is now Prospect Park and attached the other to a rock atop the Canadian cliff. Guy lines, anchored to the riverbanks, stiffened all but the middle fifty feet of the rope, dangling 190 feet above the deep green water.

More than twenty thousand people came to watch. Blondin started across from the American side, a lean man five feet, four inches tall, wearing spangled pink tights and carrying a twenty-eight-foot pole for balance. Halfway across, he paused to sit on the rope. Closer to the Canadian cliff, he turned a somersault. When he finally set foot in Canada, a band played *La Marseillaise*, the French national anthem.

After a short rest, Blondin started back across the rope. But instead of a balance pole, he carried a camera and a tripod. Two hundred feet from the Canadian cliff, he stopped to photograph the American spectators.

Blondin spent the next two summers entertaining the Niagara crowds. Every crossing was unique. He walked backwards across the rope, he crossed blindfolded, then shackled, then pushing a wheelbarrow. On one trip, he pulled a bottle of champagne up from the *Maid of the Mist* with a rope; on another, he wheeled a stove onto the rope and cooked an omelet. August 19, 1859, he crossed the gorge carrying his manager, Harry Colcord, on his back (according to an 1862 biography, Blondin told Colcord to "sit quiet, or I shall have to put you down.").

In the summer of 1860, Albert Edward, the Prince of Wales, spent four months visiting Canada and the United States. He toured the White House and George Washington's Mount Vernon with President James Buchanan and laid the cornerstone for Ottawa's Parliament Hill. On September 14, he attended Blondin's last performance at Niagara Falls. After offering to carry the Prince across on the rope, Blondin outdid himself by crossing the gorge on stilts. When he reached the opposite site, the future King Edward VII said, "Thank God it is all over!"

Billed as "The Hero of Niagara," Blondin continued performing until 1896, when he was seventy-two years old (he died in bed the following year, of diabetes). At London's Crystal Palace, he recreated many of his Niagara stunts in front of a painting of the falls, wearing a costume decorated with American Indian beadwork (on at least one occasion, he also wore a feathered headdress).

Later in the nineteenth century, several other ropewalkers tempted fate at Niagara. Italian circus performer Maria Spelterini repeated many of Blondin's stunts on a rope north of Roebling's suspension bridge in 1876. Stephen Peer, who grew up near Niagara Falls, made one successful crossing in 1887, but then fell to his death three days later. Authorities on both sides of the river banned ropewalking in 1896, after twenty-one-year-old James Hardy became the youngest person to cross the gorge.

No exceptions were granted until 2012, when—after two years of planning and legal battles—Nik Wallenda received permission to walk over the Horseshoe Fall from Goat Island to Table Rock. For eleven days, he rehearsed in the parking lot of the Seneca Niagara Casino, using fire hoses and giant fans to simulate the wind and spray. He began the actual crossing at 10:16 pm on Friday, June 15. Cranes on either side of the river supported an eight-and-a-half-ton steel cable, two inches in diameter and eighteen hundred feet long. At the insistence of ABC Television, which helped fund the event and aired it live for an estimated thirteen million viewers, Wallenda broke with family tradition and wore a safety harness. After twenty-five minutes in the wind and mist, he stepped down onto Canadian soil to the cheers of 125,000 spectators… and presented his passport to the waiting customs officials.

Nik Wallenda is a seventh-generation circus performer, who began his ropewalking career when he was thirteen. His ancestors began touring the Austro-Hungarian Empire in the 1780s, and John Ringling invited the family to join "The Greatest Show on Earth" in the 1920s.

Did you know?

Nineteenth-century ropewalkers were called "Funambulists," from the Latin words for "rope" and "walk."

Magician and escape artist Harry Houdini produced and starred in several silent movies in the early 1920s. He performed most of his own stunts, including a dangerous rescue on the edge of the American Falls in *The Man From Beyond* (1922). Fellow magician David Copperfield, owner of the world's largest collection of Houdini illusions and props, appeared to go over the Horseshoe Fall on a burning raft for the finale of his 1990 television special, *The Niagara Falls Challenge*.

The **Seneca Niagara Casino** opened in Niagara Falls, New York in 2002. The hotel tower was completed in 2005.

ANNIE EDSON TAYLOR was sixty-two years old in the summer of 1901, tired of searching for teaching jobs and ready to retire in style. As crowds gathered in Buffalo for the Pan American Exposition, she decided to seek her fame and fortune at Niagara Falls.

With the help of Michigan carnival promoter Frank Russell, Taylor ordered an oak barrel, four and half feet high and three feet in diameter. She placed a mattress inside for padding, leather straps to hold her in place, and a two-hundred-pound anvil to keep the barrel upright in the water. After Russell displayed the contraption in Michigan, Taylor announced that she would ride it over Niagara Falls on October 24—her sixty-third birthday.

Two days before taking the plunge, Taylor sent a cat over in the barrel, to prove the stunt was survivable. On the scheduled afternoon, she climbed inside and fastened the straps. Her assistants secured the lid, used a bicycle pump to fill the barrel with compressed air, and then hammered a cork into the air hole. At five minutes past four, they set the barrel adrift south of Goat Island.

Eighteen minutes later, thousands of spectators watched it drop off the edge of the Horseshoe.

Another seventeen minutes would pass before it was dragged onto the Canadian shore, where Annie Taylor emerged, shaken and bruised but without serious injury. To the waiting reporters, she said, "nobody ought ever to do that again."

The stunt made her famous, but never wealthy. Her manager and promoter, Frank Russell, stole the barrel, and Taylor spent most of her savings trying to recover it. In her later years, the "Heroine of Niagara Falls" earned her living posing for pictures with tourists at a souvenir stand near the falls. When she died in 1921, at the age of eighty-three, Annie Taylor was buried in Oakwood Cemetery, in Niagara Falls, New York. Her stone reads, "First to go over the Horseshoe Fall in a Barrel and Live."

Many daredevils have since ignored Taylor's advice, and attempted to go over the falls in barrels or even on jet skis. Some have survived, others have lost their lives. It's now illegal to try; surviving may or may not make you famous, but it will probably get you locked up or fined.

The **Horseshoe Fall** is 176 feet high and 2,600 feet wide (photographed from Terrapin Point on Goat Island).

Did you know?

Chris Van Allsburg, the author and illustrator of *The Polar Express* and *Jumanji*, introduced Annie Edson Taylor to a new generation of children with his 2011 book *Queen of the Falls*.

1901 publicity photo of **Annie Edson Taylor**.

Chapter Twelve
Preserving Niagara

ON FEBRUARY 8, 1882, OSCAR WILDE gave an afternoon lecture in Buffalo. Afterwards, he rode a train to Niagara Falls: "a vast amount of water going the wrong way and then falling over unnecessary rocks." Though he would later write of the falls' "majestic splendor and strength ... far beyond what I had ever seen in Europe," Wilde found nothing to praise in the busy tourist towns that had grown up around them:

> Niagara is a melancholy place filled with melancholy people, who wander about trying to get up that feeling of sublimity, which the guide-books assure them they can do without extra charge.

By 1882, that "feeling of sublimity" was almost the only thing at Niagara that came "without extra charge." Visitors did not have to pay to see the falls from the Canadian side, because the government still owned all the land in the old military "chain reserve." But to get there, you had to pass through a carnival midway, crowded with booths and tents and stalls, loud with barkers and street performers and eager hack drivers.

Samuel Davis owned some of the most valuable property, opposite Goat Island near the top of the Horseshoe Fall. Thomas Barnett had built a museum there in 1827, and then a stairway to the riverbank. For decades, the most adventurous sightseers had been scrambling over spray-swept rocks to explore a narrow path behind the Canadian edge of the Horseshoe (fifteen or twenty yards in, "Termination Rock" blocked the way). "Do not forget to carry a pint of brandy with you," John Maude had written, "and some dry clothes." Barnett made the trail a popular attraction by hiring guides to take paying groups of visitors "Behind the Sheet." Davis, who built the Table Rock Hotel alongside Barnett's museum in 1853, quickly added a competing stairway.

Competition turned to warfare when Davis built a stone wall to block Barnett's access to the gorge. Over the next two decades, several stairways "mysteriously" burned. Davis's supporters threw debris from the top of the gorge down onto Barnett's customers. Barnett's friends attacked Davis's son Edward with sticks and stones, and then cried murder when the young man shot one of them in self-defense (he was acquitted at trial). The feud ended in 1877, after Barnett declared bankruptcy and Davis bought his property and attractions at auction.

On the American side, every property from which the falls could be seen was privately owned and closed off with fences or walls. Admission to each ranged from twenty-five cents to a dollar or more, with extra fees charged for various "attractions" ranging from museums to comedy theaters.

The stone **Terrapin Tower** stood on the American edge of the Horseshoe Fall from 1829 until 1873 and can be seen in several paintings by Frederic Church. (This photograph, by John P. Soule, was first published as part of the *American Views* series of stereoscopic slides.)

Because there was no impressive overhang like Table Rock on the American side, the Porter brothers had built one in 1817: a three-hundred-foot wooden footbridge from Goat Island to Terrapin Rock, on the edge of the Horseshoe. The structure continued another ten feet over the brink, creating what Peter A. Porter later described as, "an absolutely unique and dangerous point of observation."

In 1829, Parkhurst Whitney built Niagara's first observation tower on Terrapin Rock. Forty feet tall, with a stairway inside and a narrow wooden gallery at the top, the Terrapin Tower looked like a small lighthouse standing watch on the edge of the world.

That same year, the Porters built an enclosed spiral staircase from the crest of Goat Island to the hundred-foot high mound of rubble below. They named it the Biddle Stairs, after the man who financed it: Nicholas Biddle, president of the Second Bank of the United States. Eighty feet tall, with small windows for light, the Biddle Stairs survived nearly a century of Niagara winters.

For most of that time, they provided the only access to one of the area's most popular attractions. In 1834, a local man had discovered a tall, shallow cavern behind the Bridal Veil Fall, the narrow cascade between Goat and Luna Islands. By the 1840s, visitors were paying a dollar apiece for guided tours of "The Cave of the Winds."

Except for these few simple attractions, the Porter family kept their islands mostly undeveloped. But they gradually sold off their land on the riverbank, until mills and hotels crowded the rapids. In 1872, they sold Prospect Point, which Peter A. Porter later mourned as "the last spot of land on the American shore from which a near view of the falls could be obtained." (As part of this transaction, the Porters also agreed to demolish the old Terrapin Tower, so it would not compete with the Point's attractions. Visitors were told it had become unsafe.)

The new owners quickly walled and "improved" their property, creating the nineteenth-century equivalent of a theme park. After the State of New York acquired Prospect Point, landscape architects Frederick Law Olmsted and Calvert Vaux condemned the park's artificial island and stream, the pavilions, faux ruins, and "a quantity of theatrical machinery for decorating the Great Fall with red, white, and blue lights."

> What was the purpose of these improvements? It was to draw visitors by any means to a particular piece of ground where money could be made out of them, and to so occupy them when there that they should not wish to go elsewhere. In this respect, the improvements were so far a success...

And then there were the hack drivers, waiting outside all the train stations and hotels on both sides of the river. Get in the cab and ask to see the falls, and the driver would take you to some other "point of interest" miles away. Sometimes admission was charged on the way in; other times, no fee would be mentioned until the visitors had already seen whatever there was to see and were ready to leave. Either way, the driver received a percentage of the fee; and if there was a store on the property—there usually was—he also got a commission on sales. Eventually, after scoring all the commissions he thought his passengers could afford, he would deliver them to some point with a view of the falls.

Visitors watching the American Falls from **Prospect Point**.

Travel writer David Young warned tourists about these tricks in his 1884 book *The Humbugs of Niagara Falls Exposed.* Subtitled "A Complete Tourist's Guide, giving hints that will enable the visitor to avoid imposition," the book included a promise from the publisher that, "There is no person permitted to advertise in this volume for whose reliability we cannot vouch." Young explained the commissions, listed admission fees and reasonable cab fares, and warned that many hotel owners would only direct visitors to attractions in which they had a financial interest. He also recommended that visitors "adopt the English custom and walk. The distance between the various points of interest is not great, the walks from one place to another are pleasant and safe, and the scenery unsurpassed."

Though designed to save tourists money, the book also addressed a problem for many Niagara Falls business owners. "Swindling has become more systematic," Young wrote in the introduction, and "is gradually driving visitors from the place..." By the early 1880s, the number of visitors was dropping every year. The wealthy travelers who once filled the grand hotels had already moved on to less commercialized places. Now the middle- and working-class tourists, hearing how expensive Niagara had become, were looking for somewhere cheaper to spend their holidays.

PAINTER FREDERIC EDWIN CHURCH was the son of a wealthy Hartford, Connecticut silversmith and watchmaker. At eighteen, he began studying at the Catskill, New York studio of Thomas Cole, founder of the Hudson River School of landscape painting. Five years later, Church became the youngest associate ever elected to the National Academy of Design.

Church often spent the warmer months traveling and sketching, and his winters painting. He painted Hudson River and New England scenes, but also South American, European, and Middle Eastern landscapes. In 1856, he sketched Niagara Falls.

The following year, Church held a one-painting show at a New York City gallery. The painting, simply titled *Niagara*, was more than seven feet long and three feet high and showed the Horseshoe Fall from Canada. Art critics raved, and in just two weeks, more than a hundred thousand people paid a quarter apiece to see it; some of them also ordered chromolithograph copies. The painting traveled widely—up and down the east coast, twice through Britain, and across the Channel to Paris for the 1867 *Exposition Universelle*—before finding a permanent home at the Corcoran Gallery in Washington, D.C. in 1876. Church also painted the falls from the American side, and a winter scene of Goat Island and the Terrapin Tower. In the 1860s, he began speaking publicly about the need to preserve the land around the falls, before it was all developed.

Frederick Hamilton-Temple-Blackwood, better known as Lord Dufferin, served as Governor-General of Canada from 1872-78 (he would later spend four years as Viceroy and Governor-General of India). Church visited him with *New York World* editor William Hurlburt to discuss the possibility of establishing an international park, to preserve the views on both sides of the falls. Dufferin visited Niagara in 1873, staying at the Clifton House, and then began promoting the park idea within his government.

In 1880, the Ontario Legislature passed "An Act Respecting Niagara Falls and the Adjacent Territory," encouraging the "Government or Parliament of Canada" to begin acquiring the necessary lands. After five years of inaction, the Legislature passed a second act, beginning:

> Whereas, the Government of the Dominion of Canada has not availed itself of the provisions of the Act passed in the forty-third year of her Majesty's reign ... it is desirable that other means should be taken to restore, to some extent, the scenery around the Falls of Niagara to its natural condition, and to preserve the same from further deterioration, and to afford travelers and others facilities for observing the points of interest in the vicinity...

With the 1885 Act, the Legislature created the Niagara Parks Commission. Sir Casimir Gzowski—designer of the International Railway Bridge—was appointed president. The Commission then purchased 154 acres along the river and gorge, stretching nearly two miles from the head of the rapids to below the falls. Total cost: $436,813.24.

Gzowski designed the new Queen Victoria Niagara Falls Park, supervising the removal of unwanted buildings and the construction of scenic walks and a carriage drive. The park opened on the Queen's birthday—May 24, 1888—but the Commission's work was just beginning. Today it maintains 3,274 acres, along the entire length of the Niagara River.

Construction of the scenic Niagara Parkway, which runs from Fort Erie to Lake Ontario, began in 1908. The southern section opened in 1912. The Parkway reached the Whirlpool in 1915 and was completed in 1931. Twelve years later, Sir Winston Churchill called it "the prettiest Sunday afternoon drive in the world." The Niagara River Recreation Trail, a walking and cycling path, runs alongside for thirty-three miles.

From the start, the Commission was required to be self-supporting, paying its bills with fees and rentals. To increase revenue from Thomas Barnett's old "Behind the Sheet" attraction, the Commission replaced the stairway in 1887, with a ten-passenger hydraulic lift. Two years later, a rock fall at the center of the Horseshoe shifted the flow of water, leaving the once-hidden path exposed and dry.

Built in 1904, **Queen Victoria Place** is one of the oldest buildings in Queen Victoria Park. The restaurant inside was first called the Refectory, and then the Victoria Park Restaurant; today it is known as Edgewater's.

Though visitors are no longer able to walk directly behind the Horseshoe, it is still possible to see the back of the fall from the Canadian side. In 1902, the Niagara Parks Commission gave its hydraulic lift to the Ontario Power Company, which used it to carry workers down to the riverbank. In return, the Power Company built a new elevator and dug a "scenic tunnel" through the stone and clay, so visitors could look out at the falling water. A larger, concrete-lined tunnel was dug farther back from the fall in 1944, erosion having made the original unsafe. Along with the outdoor observation deck added in 1951, the attraction is now billed as "Journey Behind the Falls."

In their 1889 report, the Commissioners, "after carefully considering the question are forced to admit that even with improved conditions the source from which the revenues are now drawn will prove inadequate to meet the annual cost of maintaining the park ..." Two years later, for an annual rent of ten thousand dollars, they allowed the Niagara Falls Park and River Railway Company to lay tracks in the park and to build a direct current generating station near the Horseshoe. Early in the twentieth century, the Commission granted licenses for three more generating stations, two above the Horseshoe and one at the foot of the cliff, below Queen Victoria Park.

In 1887, the Niagara Parks Commission bought a group of small islands and named them after Lord Dufferin. Located on the Canadian side of the river, a little more than a mile above the falls, the Dufferin Islands are connected by bridges, and are brightly decorated every winter for the "Festival of Lights."

FREDERICK LAW OLMSTED and Calvert Vaux began designing parks for Buffalo in 1868. The following year, Olmsted met Parkhurst Whitney, Peter Porter, and other Niagara businessmen at the Cataract House to discuss ways to preserve the scenery around the falls. Olmsted was especially concerned about the fate of Goat Island, for which the Porter family had received a variety of tempting offers. Jim Fiske wanted the island for a railroad terminal, the Vanderbilts hoped to build a resort there, and P.T. Barnum had considered it as a permanent home for his circus. Olmsted believed the islands, and the other viewing spots on the mainland, should be preserved in their natural state, and that they should be free to visit.

Despite the best efforts of Olmsted, Church, and many others, no official action was taken in New York until 1879. In a January address to the State Assembly, Governor Lucius Robinson spoke of the need for an international park around the falls. In response, the legislators asked the Commissioners of the State Survey to look into the matter. Over the next year, Survey director James Gardner worked with Olmsted to prepare a detailed report, illustrated with photographs of the damage that had already been done.

By the time the report was submitted, in March 1880, Alonzo Barton Cornell was sitting in the governor's chair. Determined to cut government spending, Cornell vetoed as many appropriations bills as he could. The Survey report did not move him, nor did a petition submitted by Olmsted and signed by such luminaries as Charles Darwin, Ralph Waldo Emerson, and Henry Wadsworth Longfellow. Bills for preserving Niagara were shot down in the Legislature in 1880 and 1881. The next year, no attempt was made.

Though New York's next governor, Grover Cleveland, supported the preservation effort, many in government remained opposed. Unlike Ontario, New York had no government-owned "Chain Reserve" on which to build a park. All the land the "reservationists" wanted to open to the public was privately owned, and some legislators estimated that buying it would cost between five and ten million dollars.

Luckily, Niagara also had a fierce advocate in Albany. Thomas Welch, born in 1850, had grown up in the town of Niagara Falls. He owned a dry goods store there, and had been town clerk, a town trustee, and town supervisor. He was elected to the New York State Assembly in 1880, after spending two years as Niagara County's chairman of the board.

Bridge from Goat Island to the Three Sisters' Islands.

In 1883, while Olmsted and others promoted their cause in the New York and Boston newspapers, Welch championed the proposed Reservation in the Assembly. "(T)he state of things existing at Niagara," he said, "with the cataract enclosed for private profit, does not reflect credit on the State or the nation which boasts of its possession."

> If Providence had placed Niagara in England or France, in Germany, in Italy, or in any of the great States of Europe—which send their thousands here every year to gaze upon it,—we know that the great cataract would not be permitted for a moment to be private property. It should be taken by the State at once, and held as its most precious possession

Cascades between the Three Sisters' Islands.

Welch then dismissed the inflated estimates for the cost of the land, much of which the state could condemn by right of eminent domain. Arguing that, "there is hardly a citizen of this State who does not hope to visit Niagara during his lifetime," he went on to show the true cost of buying the property: about thirty-six cents out of the taxes of the average New Yorker, a few dollars for the wealthiest citizens.

> ...can he view the spectacle to its full extant for the sums which I have shown would be his share of taxation for the proposed State Reservation? Under the present order of things, I venture to say it would cost him ten times that amount, and he will be required to pay it on every succeeding occasion.

On April 30, 1883, Governor Cleveland signed "An Act to authorize the selection, location, and appropriation of certain lands in the Village of Niagara Falls for a State Reservation, and to preserve the scenery of the Falls of Niagara." To accomplish these goals, the Act created a five-member Niagara Reservation Commission.

Andrew Haswell Green was appointed president, a title he would hold until his death in 1903. Born in Worcester, Massachusetts in 1820, Green came to New York as a young man to study law. Few have done more to improve their adopted home. He worked with Olmsted and Vaux in the 1850s and 1860s to create Central Park and was one of the founders of the Metropolitan Museum of Art, the American Museum of Natural History, the New York Public Library, and the Bronx Zoo. In 1895, he founded the American Scenic and Historical Preservation Society, which would soon join the fight to save the Hudson River Palisades from quarry operators. And in 1898, he finally succeeded—after twenty years of negotiating—in bringing Manhattan, Brooklyn, Queens, Staten Island, and the Bronx together as "Greater New York." (That same year, Niagara's Bath Island—no longer occupied by a sprawling paper mill—was renamed "Green Island.")

The Commissioners chose 107 acres to preserve, including all of Goat Island and the other islands near the falls; the shoreline along the American rapids; and the American side of the gorge from the falls to Prospect Point. Some legislators considered the appraised value of the land—$1,433,429.50—excessive, but after another round of newspaper campaigning by Olmsted and the other Reservationists, Governor David Bennett Hill signed the appropriation bill on April 30, 1885 (Hill had been Grover Cleveland's lieutenant governor; he took over as governor when Cleveland won the 1884 presidential election, and was then reelected in 1885 and 1888). Fences, walls, and the most unsightly buildings were quickly removed, and the Niagara Reservation was opened to the public on July 15. For the first time in decades, visitors could see the falls from the American side for free.

In 1887, Olmsted and Vaux presented a detailed report on how the Reservation property could best be preserved in—or restored to—something like its natural state. Along the shoreline, "the canals and excavations [should be] filled, all the waterside crib-work and walls removed." The islands should be left in their wooded state, and all park-like features should be removed or refused:

> Suppose, for instance, that a costly object of art, like that of the Statue of Liberty, should be tendered to the State on condition that it should be set upon Goat Island ... our argument ... would oblige a declension of the gift as surely as it would the refusal of an offer to stock the island with poison ivy or with wolves or bears.

Olmsted and Vaux also believed that, in order to maintain the natural scenery, "Some visitors must even be condemned to what they will think something of a hardship at certain points." For example, they did not believe there was any need to build refreshment stands, because "there is no point in the reservation ... that is more than ten minutes' walk or five minutes' drive from hotels and restaurants standing on land of private ownership."

The entrance to **Niagara Reservation** (Niagara Falls State Park), at the intersection of Prospect and Old Falls Streets in Niagara Falls, New York.

As Superintendent of the Niagara Reservation during its first eighteen years, Thomas Welch followed at least the outlines of the Olmsted / Vaux plan. Many of the details, however, were abandoned during the twentieth century. Roads, parking lots, and pavilions have been added, along with flowerbeds, statuary, and other monuments. In the 1960s, the four-lane Robert Moses Parkway was driven through the Reservation property (this stretch of the highway was removed in the 1980s).

Terrapin Point on Goat Island, overlooking the Horseshoe Fall.

Goat Island has also been twice enlarged with landfill. In 1953, the river was filled between the island and the Terrapin Rocks on the American edge of the Horseshoe. (By 1969, cracks had formed. Terrapin Point was closed to visitors until September 1983, when the Army Corps of Engineers finished blasting away unstable rock and building new retaining walls). In the 1960s, the east end of the island was extended for parking lots and a heliport.

Several existing attractions, including the Cave of the Winds and the Prospect Park Incline Railway, were incorporated into the Reservation. The Cave of the Winds tours behind the Bridal Veil Fall were discontinued in 1920, after a rock fall killed three visitors and injured several others. In 1924, guides began leading visitors in front of the fall, rather than behind it.

An elevator opened the following year, and the old Biddle Stairs were demolished in 1927.

Though the name "Cave of the Winds" is still used, the cave no longer exists; the overhang was dynamited in 1955, after several visitors were injured by a rockslide. The modern attraction consists of redwood boardwalks, stairs, and observation decks in front of the Bridal Veil. The closest approach is the "Hurricane Deck," twenty feet from the cascade and swept by sixty-eight mile-an-hour winds. All of the structures are removed each winter, to prevent them behind crushed by the ice tumbling over the falls.

Parkhurst Whitney had built the Inclined Railway in 1845. Two tracks, covered by a roof, sloped to the foot of the gorge. The sightseeing cable-cars were counterbalanced, so that as one descended, the other rose (there was also a 250-step stairway, for anyone who preferred to walk). In the 1860s, Whitney built the "Shadow of the Rock" complex at the foot of the railway, including changing rooms and a covered walkway to an observation deck beside the American Fall.

Ice destroyed the Shadow of the Rock buildings in 1892. The State replaced them with a pavilion modeled after a Swiss chalet, which lasted until July 6, 1907, when the railway's cable snapped. The railcars crashed into the building. One visitor was killed; several others were injured and rushed to the Canadian shore aboard the *Maid of the Mist*. The railway was shut down, and then replaced in 1910 with an elevator drilled straight down through the rock from Prospect Point to the foot of the gorge.

The **Cave of the Winds** boardwalks and viewing decks, at the foot of Goat Island below the Bridal Veil Fall.

The shaft started leaking in 1954, after a massive rockslide. The State closed the attraction, and then began constructing the 282-foot Prospect Point Observation Tower in 1958. Built of aluminum, glass, and steel, at a cost of $1.25 million, it opened in February 1961. Eight million visitors ride the elevators every year to board the *Maid of the Mist*, or to climb the stairways to the viewing decks near the American Falls.

Did you know?

The Niagara Reservation is the oldest of New York's 179 State Parks and was the United States' first state park.

Luna Island, which separates the American and Bridal Veil Falls, is 150 feet wide and 350 feet long. The name refers to the "moon bows"—faint lunar cousins of rainbows—which early visitors sometimes saw from the island (today they are obscured by the electric lights all around the falls).

Right: The **Prospect Point Observation Tower** opened in Niagara Falls State Park in 1961. The Rainbow Bridge to Canada is visible in the background.

The **Cave of the Winds** elevator building, on Goat Island.

EARLY IN THE TWENTIETH CENTURY, preservationists faced a new battle. Every second of the year, electric companies were diverting thousands of cubic feet of water from the Upper Niagara to drive their turbines. Though this water was eventually returned to the river below the falls, every diversion meant less water flowing *over* Niagara Falls.

"The objections to using this power instead of allowing it to run to waste are sentimental and poetic," wrote Elbert Hubbard, founder of the Roycroft artisan community, in 1914.

If it could be arranged to utilize all the water at Niagara Falls for industrial purposes for six days in the week, and then, on the seventh, to turn the water on ... we will see the Falls for a few hours, just as Father Hennepin saw them.

In 1950, the United States and Canada signed the Niagara Diversion Treaty, specifying how much water each nation could draw from the river for power generation. To preserve the appearance of Niagara Falls, the treaty required that, between eight in the morning and ten at night, from April to October, a minimum of 100,000 cubic feet of water had to pass over the falls every second. After ten, and in the winter when fewer people visited, the total was reduced to 50,000 cubic feet per second—less than a third of the river's volume. The rest was divided evenly between the American and Canadian power industries.

The modern appearance of Niagara Falls is the result of various efforts to slow erosion at the center of the Horseshoe and to maintain the illusion of a historic amount of water tumbling into the gorge. The width of the Horseshoe was reduced by four hundred feet in the 1980s, and much of the river's water is diverted from the center of the crest to the edges, where it makes the most impression on visitors. In 1969, water was diverted entirely from the American Falls, so the Army Corps of Engineers could drill drainage holes to slow erosion and stabilize the cliffs.

The **International Control Works** was built by the New York Power Authority and Ontario Power Generation between 1954 and 1961, to regulate the flow of water over Niagara Falls. Operated by the International Niagara Control Board, it stretches more than eighteen hundred feet from the Canadian shore.

Did you know?

Before William Forsyth and Parkhurst Whitney built stairways to the riverbanks in 1818, visitors who wanted to look up at the falls climbed down with the help of ropes or—on the Canadian side—precarious ladders. One of the first was called the "Indian Ladder:" two straight trees with notches cut every twelve or fifteen inches for hand- and footholds.

Chapter Thirteen
Harnessing Niagara

WILLOW ISLAND, NAMED for a riverfront grove, used to be on the American side of the Niagara River, opposite Goat Island. All that separated it from the mainland was a narrow canal, which visitors crossed on a stone bridge. During the construction of the Robert Moses State Parkway in the early 1960s, the canal was filled in. Willow Island became part of the shoreline, and the earliest known attempt to harness Niagara's power became a memory.

Daniel Joncaire, the French soldier and fur trader who built Little Fort Niagara, dug the canal in 1759 to power a sawmill. John Stedman rebuilt the mill after the French and Indian War and ran it until the British abandoned their western forts in the 1790s. Augustus Porter bought the property from New York in 1805, and then enlarged the canal to drive his gristmill and tannery.

In the half-mile of rapids above the American Falls, the Niagara River drops fifty feet. The Porter brothers believed the power of these rapids could be harnessed to make Niagara Falls a major industrial center. Shortly after acquiring the river islands in 1816, they considered building mills on the eastern half of Goat Island and hotels or mansions on the west, overlooking the falls. Fortunately, nothing ever came of these plans but a large paper mill on neighboring Bath Island. Built in 1826 and enlarged several times, it was demolished after the founding of Niagara Reservation.

The Porters next tried to interest investors in a "hydraulic canal," which would carry water from above the rapids to mill sites along gorge. A Niagara Falls Hydraulic Company was finally established in 1852 but went bankrupt before completing the canal.

Horace H. Day bought the company in the late 1850s and completed the mile-long canal in 1861. Thirty-five feet wide and eight feet deep, it carried water from "Port Day" above the rapids to the edge of the cliff… where for the next ten years, it simply spilled—unused—into the gorge.

Day had made his fortune manufacturing India rubber in the 1840s and 1850s. He retired in 1859, after a long and costly legal battle with rival Charles Goodyear, who had sued him for patent infringement. At Niagara, Day bought the Hydraulic Canal property for $700,000, and then tried to recoup his investment by demanding such outrageous rents that potential customers fled to Rochester (the canal's first—and only—user was Charles Gaskill, who built a flour mill overlooking the gorge in the early 1870s).

Jacob Friedrich Schoellkopf was born in Germany in 1819, the youngest of ten children. Though his family ran a profitable tannery, he came to the United States at the age of twenty-two, learned to speak English, and settled in Buffalo. "Starting practically without capital," wrote Elbert Hubbard in *Power: or, the Story of Niagara Falls*, "he built stores, shops, tanneries, mills, and set thousands of people to work. He erected houses, laid

116

out roadways, managed banks, and growing rich himself, he made others rich, too." By the 1870s, Schoellkopf had mills in Buffalo, Milwaukee, and Chicago.

In 1877, Schoellkopf formed the Niagara Falls Hydraulic Power and Manufacturing Company with a group of investors and bought the Hydraulic Canal for less than a tenth of what Day had spent seventeen years before. Soon there were seven mills along the gorge rim, including the Schoellkopf Chemical and Dye Company. Niagara water drove the machinery, falling fifty feet through iron tubes called "penstocks" to turn wooden wheels nine feet in diameter. Within a few years, Schoellkopf had bought out his partners and reorganized Niagara Falls Hydraulic as the Schoellkopf Hydraulic Power Company.

Inventor Charles Brush, founder of the Brush Electric Company, came to Niagara Falls in 1881. For twenty years, showmen had been illuminating the falls after dark with short-lived—but very expensive—calcium flares. Brush offered to light the falls—and the main streets of Niagara Falls, New York—with electric arc lamps, powered by a dynamo of his own design. Schoellkopf built a larger penstock to deliver an eighty-six foot "head" of water, which smashed the first wheel placed under it. The installation of a sturdier wheel made the experiment a success and put Schoellkopf in the electric power business.

Brush went on to light the streets of cities from New York to San Francisco, before increasing competition from Thomas Edison's incandescent lamps forced him to sell out to his biggest rival, the Thomson-Houston Electric Company (Thomson-Houston later merged with Edison to form General Electric). In 1888, Brush built a wind turbine at his Cleveland home; it supplied all the electricity he needed until his death in

1929, even charging batteries for times when the wind wasn't blowing.

Schoellkopf built a second generating plant in 1895, on the riverbank below the manufacturing district; water fell 210 feet to turn the wheels. But as Hubbard wrote in 1914, "So fast have we traveled that the apparatus in use in 1895 has practically been abandoned." Schoellkopf's sons, who inherited the company on his death in 1899, began building a third riverbank power station in 1904. Concrete-encased penstocks poured Niagara's water over thirteen turbines, spinning them three hundred revolutions a minute.

ENGINEER THOMAS EVERSHED proposed another method of drawing power from the Niagara River in 1896, when he chartered the Niagara Falls Hydraulic Tunnel Power and Sewer Company. Born in Sussex, England in 1817, Evershed settled in Rochester, New York in 1836. He helped James Hall survey Niagara Falls in 1842, worked for several railroads, and planned and supervised the enlargement of the western part of the Erie Canal. In 1884 and 1885, he directed the surveys for the Niagara Reservation.

Thomas Evershed was also a skilled artist. In 1849, he and a group of friends traveled to California during the Gold Rush. Evershed illustrated his journal of the three-month trip with sketches, from which he painted a series of watercolors when they reached San Francisco. Later in life, he joined the Rochester Art Club, displaying many of his paintings and serving on the board of directors in 1887-88.

Evershed's company received permission from New York to draw water from the Niagara a mile above the falls, just east of the State Park. Canals would deliver it to dozens of mills, whose deep wheel pits emptied into an enormous tunnel carved through solid rock underneath the city of Niagara Falls. Two and a half miles from the intake, the water would spill back into the river near Roebling's Suspension Bridge. The Buffalo Businessmen's Association tried to fund the project with subscriptions, but little was accomplished before Evershed died in 1890.

In 1889, financier Edward Dean Adams and lawyer William Birch Rankine chartered the Cataract Construction Company as a subsidiary of the Tunnel Company. As president, Adams convinced some of America's wealthiest men, including J. P. Morgan, William Vanderbilt, and John Jacob Astor, to invest in the tunnel. In 1890, the Businessmen's Association of Niagara Falls publicized the work with a booklet titled *The Water-Power of the Falls of Niagara Applied to Manufacturing Purposes*; the lengthy subtitle promised "an accurate description of one of the greatest undertakings of the age, with plans, maps and illustrations." Inside were glowing descriptions of:

> ...lands extending two miles, along the shore of the Niagara River adjacent to the Hydraulic Tunnel, which have been laid out for lots, streets, mill races, wharves, and railway sidings for the purpose of forming a town composed wholly of mills, factories, and workshops... (and) an adjacent tract of one thousand acres, which has been laid out in streets and lots for homes for workmen...

Premature promises, of course. As another passage makes clear, the company was still trying to figure out how to use the river's power:

The water falls upon turbine wheels … and the power developed thereby will be delivered to the mills or factories at that point, *or transmitted by cable, pneumatic tube, or electricity to adjacent lands as the customers may desire.* [Italics added]

The company directors favored electricity but had to decide how to distribute it. Thomas Edison's company had been building Direct Current generating stations since 1882. The technology was proven… but direct current could not be sent more than a mile or two. Edison proposed solving this problem by building numerous local generating stations burning coal or oil. But the rushing waters of the upper Niagara would produce far more power than was needed locally, and the directors dreamed of supplying customers twenty miles away in Buffalo. Alternating current could be "stepped up" for long-distance transmission, but the technology was still mostly untested, and Edison was spending a small fortune trying to convince the public it was dangerous.

George Westinghouse was already a successful inventor and manufacturer of railroad air brakes and signals when he founded the Westinghouse Electric Company in 1884. Recognizing early the advantages of alternating current, Westinghouse negotiated exclusive licenses for the Serbian inventor Nikola Tesla's polyphase induction motors and transformers (Westinghouse would later hire Tesla as a researcher).

Westinghouse proved that alternating current was both practical and safe in 1893, when he lit the entire Chicago World's Fair. Impressed by his results, the directors of the Cataract Construction Company hired him to build three huge generators, plus transformers and 11,000-volt transmission cables.

To house the turbines, Evershed's old company—renamed the Niagara Falls Power Company—built Power House No. 1 a mile and a half above the falls. A short intake canal let water into the plant from above the American Rapids. To return it to the river below the falls, the company built a brick-lined tunnel seven thousand feet long, 160 feet beneath the growing city (the outlet was just north of Prospect Park). The generators were turned on August 26, 1895, and on November 15, 1896, the Edward Dean Adams Power Station began transmitting electricity to Buffalo. Power House No. 2 was completed in 1904, doubling the station's capacity.

Adams' Niagara Falls Power Company merged with the Schoellkopfs' Hydraulic Power in 1918. By 1926, the Adams power houses had been switched to standby status, so more water could be diverted to the larger Schoellkopf works on the riverbank.

On the morning of June 7, 1956, cracks appeared in the back wall of the third Schoellkopf plant. Five that afternoon, a landslide swept more than half of the concrete and steel building into the river, killing one worker, and smashing six massive generators.

The sudden loss of New York's largest hydroelectric plant sparked a fierce debate over how Niagara's power should be harnessed and distributed: by profit-driven private companies, or by a publicly owned utility? Congress settled the matter with the 1957 Niagara Redevelopment Act, which gave the New York Power Authority full use of the American share of the river's bounty.

THIS IS THE ORIGINAL ARCH ENTRANCE TO THE ADAMS STATION, THE WORLD'S FIRST HYDROELECTRIC POWER PLANT.

After the **Edward Dean Adams Power Stations** were demolished in 1961, the entrance arch from Power Station No. 1 was reassembled on Goat Island.

Right: In front of the arch sits a statue of inventor **Nikola Tesla**, by sculptor Frano Kršinić, which the government of Yugoslavia donated to the United States in 1976.

NEW YORK GOVERNOR Charles Evans Hughes first suggested creating a state-run electrical authority in 1907. The Legislature dismissed the idea as too costly, the same answer Governor Alfred E. Smith would receive in the 1920s. Governor Franklin Roosevelt finally signed the bill creating the Power Authority in 1931, with plants to build a major hydroelectric plant on the Saint Lawrence River.

Work on the station was delayed until 1954, when the New York Power Authority teamed with Canada's Ontario Hydro to build a 3,212-foot dam between New York's Barnhart Island and the Canadian shore. When the Moses-Saunders dam was completed in 1959, two years ahead of schedule, water from a hundred-square mile reservoir spun thirty-two turbines. Half of them generated electricity for the St. Lawrence-Franklin D. Roosevelt Power Project in Massena, New York; the rest for the R. H. Saunders-St. Lawrence Station in Cornwall, Ontario.

The dam was named after the two men who made Roosevelt's dream a reality: New York Power Authority chairman Robert Moses, and Ontario Hydro chairman Robert H. Saunders. Known for several decades as New York's "Master Builder," Moses was a tireless (if controversial) builder of roads, bridges, and city and state parks. Saunders was a former Toronto mayor, chosen in 1948 to lead Canada's publicly owned power utility.

With Moses in charge, the New York Power Authority began building a new Niagara Falls power plant in 1958. Unlike previous stations, it was located more than four miles north of the falls, directly across the river from Ontario Hydro's massive Sir Adam Beck Generating Stations. To make room for a structure 1,840 feet long and 580 wide, twelve million cubic yards of rock were blasted from the gorge wall; most of the rubble was then crushed to make concrete.

The Robert Moses Niagara Hydroelectric Power Station was activated on January 1, 1961. At the time, it was the world's largest hydro plant, with thirteen turbines producing a total of 2.4 million kilowatts.

It was also one of Moses's last big projects. He had given up his New York City appointments in 1959, to accept the presidency of the 1964-65 New York World's Fair. In 1962, he resigned from his state positions following a disagreement with Governor Nelson Rockefeller. Despite his achievements, many New Yorkers were glad to see him go.

Early in his career, Moses was often depicted as a hero. A 1939 *Atlantic* profile mentioned his combative nature, but focused on the playgrounds, parks, and highways he had built, and how he had transformed a Long Island garbage dump into the home of the 1939 New York World's Fair. But in 1974, Robert Caro won the Pulitzer for his critical 1,200-page biography, *The Power Broker: Robert Moses and the Fall of New York*. Caro gave Moses credit for his early successes, but also showed how he callously destroyed whole neighborhoods to carve a path for the Cross Bronx Expressway.

Water for the Power Station—375,000 gallons every second—is drawn from the upper Niagara, two and a half miles above the falls. Two enormous tunnels carry it under the city to an artificial lake, or fore bay, behind the station. At the opposite end of this fore bay is the Lewiston Pump-Generating Plant, with twelve additional turbines.

This turbine from the **Robert Moses Power Station** is displayed outside the Power Vista. Open seven days a week, year-round, this visitor's center includes more than fifty exhibits, including a history of the Tuscarora Indian Nation and a detailed scale model of the Niagara region, with lights and narration explaining how the power station works. The outdoor observation decks offer impressive views of the Robert Moses and Sir Adam Beck Generating Stations, the Lewiston-Queenston Bridge, and the Niagara Gorge.

When electricity is in lower demand, power from the Moses station is used to pump water uphill into the nineteen-hundred-acre reservoir behind the Lewiston plant. The Lewiston pumps are reversed when demand rises. Functioning now as turbines, they generate electricity as the stored water spills back into the fore bay, on its way to the penstocks of the larger Moses plant.

To build the reservoir, the Power Authority tried to claim 1,350 acres of the 6,300-acre Tuscarora Indian Reservation. Smallest of the Six Nations of the Iroquois Confederacy, the Tuscarora had supported the American cause in both the Revolution and the War of 1812. Their reservation consisted of land given them by the Seneca, the Holland Land Company, and—in 1803—the federal government.

Lead by Chief Clinton Rickard, founder of the Indian Defense League, the Tuscarora fought all the way to the Supreme Court. The 1960 decision was a compromise: the Court ruled that the Power Authority could purchase 550 acres, at a cost of fifteen hundred dollars an acre.

This bronze statue of Tuscarora Chief **Clinton Rickard** (1882-1971) has been greeting visitors to Niagara Falls State Park since 1975 (in the 1960s, Rickard—whose native name meant "Loud Voice"—often wore traditional buckskins and feathers to public events). Rickard served in the US Cavalry in the Philippines and was one of ten soldiers assigned to guard Theodore Roosevelt during a 1901 visit to Buffalo. In 1926, Rickard started the Indian Defense League, to protect the right of Native Americans to travel freely throughout North America. The plaque below the statue preserves one of his later speeches, in which he said, "My experience through more than eighty years has taught me that people of good will of all races can work together to bring about justice for all and the betterment of mankind."

The **Robert Moses Niagara Hydroelectric Power Station** in Lewiston, New York, photographed from the Power Vista.

New York Power Authority **water intake towers**, Niagara Falls, New York.

Chapter Fourteen
Industrial Niagara

ELECTRICITY QUICKLY MADE NIAGARA FALLS, New York into the industrial city imagined by the early canal builders. Paper and lumber, milled from Michigan trees, flowed from the city, along with acetylene lamps, bookbinding machinery, business forms, suspenders, metal clothing fasteners, flame-resistant Composite Board for railcar and marine interiors, and 90,000 barrels a year of lager beer and ale (at least until 1920, when Prohibition closed the Niagara Falls Brewing Company).

One company became almost as famous for its factory—which welcomed 100,000 visitors every year—as for its products. In 1893, Omaha lawyer and health-food advocate Henry Perky teamed up with William Ford, a machinist from Watertown, New York, to build a machine for making "little whole wheat mattresses." After demonstrating their invention at the 1893 Chicago World's Fair, Perky opened shredded wheat bakeries in Boston and Worcester, Massachusetts.

In 1901, Perky moved his Natural Food Company to Niagara Falls, where he built a steel-framed factory 463 feet long beside the Niagara River. Finished with two hundred tons of marble and lit by 844 windows, it quickly became known as

Niagara's "Palace of Light." Perky retired the following year, and in 1904, the business was renamed "The Shredded Wheat Company."

According to *The Wonders of Niagara*, which the company published in 1914, "One might as well see Rome without seeing St. Peter's as to see Niagara Falls without visiting 'The Home of Shredded Wheat.'" Visitors rode electric elevators to the rooftop observatory and the thousand-seat auditorium. They were shown the wheat cleaning machines, the drying and shredding rooms, the revolving ovens, and the printing plant, "from which there constantly pours a perfect Niagara of colored cartons ... booklets, leaflets, and other advertising literature." They could eat in the cafeteria or attend "an instructive talk on the food value of the whole wheat" or "the culinary possibilities of Shredded Wheat" (the dinner Perky hosted to celebrate the factory's opening included turkey stuffing, drinks, and even ice cream made from Shredded Wheat). Tourists could even send picture postcards of the factory, just fill out the address and sign under the pre-printed message: "You certainly would like Shredded Wheat even better than you do if you could see it made."

The factory's thousand employees were treated equally well, with morning and afternoon breaks, noontime meals (free for women and girls), educational lectures, and classes in dancing, shorthand, and typewriting. They could also join the Choral Society or learn to play an instrument in the "Shredded Wheat Concert Band."

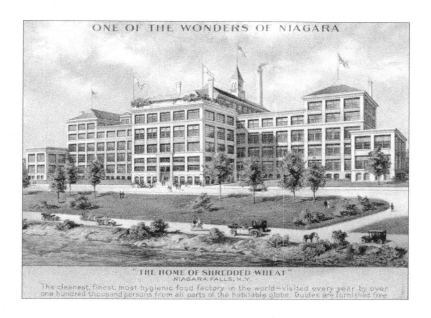

This drawing of the **Shredded Wheat Company**'s "Palace of Light" was originally printed in the 1914 edition of *The Wonders of Niagara*.

The Wonders of Niagara described Shredded Wheat as "the most perfect food that was ever devised for the nourishment of man," and included serving suggestions and recipes ("dip the Biscuit in milk, drain and fry in butter, after which it may be served with a little cream").

The **High Bank** industrial district of Niagara Falls, New York, occupied the gorge rim north of Prospect Point. At the foot of the cliff are the Schoellkopf power stations. (Postcard illustration, circa 1900)

ALTHOUGH ALUMINUM IS the most common metal in the Earth's crust, it is found only in compounds with other elements. In 1886, chemist Charles Martin Hall discovered that he could extract pure aluminum from ore using a strong electrical current (because the French scientist Paul Héroult made a similar discovery around the same time, it is called the Hall-Héroult Process). Hall joined with a group of businessmen to form the Pittsburgh Reduction Company in 1888. The company moved to Niagara Falls in 1895, and for more than fifty years, its second Niagara Plant—located directly above the Schoellkopf power houses—was the largest building on the gorge rim. As the company expanded its output, and more industries began using aluminum, the price for a pound of aluminum dropped from eight dollars in 1888 to thirty-six cents in 1897.

This section of wall on the gorge rim in Niagara Falls, New York, used to be part of the **ALCOA** aluminum plant.

Pittsburgh Reduction changed its name to the Aluminum Company of America in 1907 and is known today by the acronym ALCOA. In the first decades of the twentieth century, it was the only American company producing aluminum (and the largest aluminum company in the world); the federal government broke it up after World War Two.

At Niagara Falls, electrical processes were also used to refine other metals, including lead for storage batteries. Chemist Edward Goodrich Acheson, who helped Thomas Edison develop the incandescent lamp, built factories to electrically produce Carborundum and artificial graphite. Carborundum was the first manmade abrasive, the accidental result of Acheson's attempt to make synthetic diamonds by electrically fusing clay and carbon; today it is sold in grinding and cutting wheels, and on sanding belts, discs, and sheets. Artificial graphite was sold as a lubricant, a protective coating for iron and steel, and filler for storage batteries.

Many of Niagara's industries died out or drifted away in the second half of the twentieth century. Some left because labor was cheaper elsewhere, others because it would cost too much to update old plants or equipment. The ALCOA plant closed in 1949, and all of the factories along the Gorge rim—what had been known as the High Bank manufacturing district—were demolished in the early 1950s. Nabisco bought the Shredded Wheat Company in 1928, demolished the "Palace of Light" in 1956, and shuttered a smaller plant in 2001. The Acheson Graphite plant was demolished after the company was absorbed by Union Carbide (which started out in Niagara Falls as Acetylene Light, Heat and Power), and Carborundum left in the 1980s. In place of busy factories, Niagara was left with abandoned buildings, empty lots, and buried waste dumps.

Thomas Edison had predicted, at the turn of the century, that Niagara Falls would become "the great electro-chemical center of the world." By the 1940s, there were so many chemical companies in the city that part of Buffalo Avenue was known as "Chemical Row."

In 1942, the Hooker Chemical and Plastics Corporation bought an abandoned canal, which the city and the Army had been using as a waste dump. The company drained the canal, lined the walls with clay, and gradually filled it with twenty thousand tons of chemical waste. To contain the poisons, Hooker covered the canal with four feet of clay and topsoil.

Entrepreneur William T. Love had begun digging the canal in the 1890s. According to his brochures, it would link the

Upper Niagara to Lake Ontario. Ships would use it to bypass Niagara Falls, and hydroelectric plants would supply direct current to smokeless factories and a beautiful Model City. But Westinghouse's successes with AC made the hydro plants unnecessary, and investors bailed during the financial Panic of 1893. Love declared bankruptcy and abandoned the project after digging less than a mile. Eventually the trench filled with water. Local children used it for a swimming hole and a skating pond until the 1920s, when the city began dumping municipal waste in "Love's Canal."

When Hooker bought the canal, the land around it was undeveloped. But in the early 1950s, the city's population was still growing. The School Board offered to buy the canal property, and when the chemical company refused to sell, threatened to take the canal by condemnation. Hooker turned over the property in 1953 for one dollar, with a warning that "the premises have been filled ... with waste products resulting from the manufacturing of chemicals." The Board removed part of the canal's covering to fill a nearby property, and when it opened the 99th Street School in 1955, the playground extended over the dump.

In 1957, the School Board offered part of the canal property to housing developers. Hooker officials tried to block the sale, but the city had already begun digging sewers across the canal, piercing the clay walls. Storm drains followed, and in the early 1960s, the state's Department of Transportation damaged the canal's walls and covering while building a freeway.

Developers built more than three dozen blocks of single-family houses around the chemical dump. Most of the people who moved in were unaware of the hazard. The School Board insisted its property was safe, though children sometimes burned themselves on loose chunks of phosphorous on the playground. The city dismissed homeowners' complaints about strange smells, unexplained illnesses, and black sludge in their basements.

In 1976, melting snow and heavy rains flooded the canal and filled the sewers and drains with industrial waste. Two years later, investigative reporter Michael H. Brown began detailing the Love Canal's history in the *Niagara Falls Gazette*. Scientists identified hundreds of chemicals, many of them toxic. Health studies revealed disturbing rates of miscarriage, stillbirth, and birth defects. Homeowners and parents, led by Karen Schroeder and Lois Gibbs, declared war on the chemical company.

In August 1978, President Jimmy Carter announced that the Federal Disaster Assistance Agency—created to help victims of natural disasters—would begin relocating the affected families. Congress passed the Comprehensive Environmental Response, Compensation, and Liability Act (CERCLA) the following year; commonly known as the Superfund Act, it was the first federal program for cleaning up industrial waste.

More than eight hundred families were moved. The 99th Street School and hundreds of abandoned homes were demolished, the debris used to refill the leaking canal. New walls, caps, and monitoring stations were built, and the grass-covered canal itself—the most contaminated land—is still surrounded by a barbed-wire fence seven feet, ten inches high.

Chapter Fifteen
Canadian Power

THE FIRST HYDROELECTRIC PLANT on the Canadian side opened in 1892. Built by the owners of the new Niagara Falls and River Railway, the powerhouse shared a water intake with the City of Niagara Falls waterworks and provided direct current for the railcars traveling between Chippewa and Queenston. The Railway paid ten thousand dollars rent each year, but the Commissioners still needed another source of income to make their Park self-supporting.

Albert Duane Shaw was a Civil War veteran and a former New York State Assemblyman and had been US Consul at Toronto and at Manchester, England. In 1891, he tried to interest a group of English capitalists in building a hydroelectric station above the Horseshoe Fall. Unable to raise enough funds, he teamed with William Birch Rankine and other founders of the Niagara Falls Power Company to form the Canadian Niagara Power Company.

The Canadian Niagara Power Company's **William B. Rankine Generating Station** is located in Queen Victoria Park, alongside the Horseshoe (photographed from Goat Island).

In 1892, Canadian Niagara agreed to pay the Niagara Parks Commission an annual rent of twenty-five thousand dollars; to start building a power station by 1897; and to begin transmitting electricity in 1898. In return, the Commissioners would not grant any other licenses for power generation within the park.

As the deadline approached, Canadian Niagara's directors were still wrestling with the technical problems of transmitting power to Toronto. William Rankine asked the Ontario government for an extension of the monopoly; to fulfill the company's promise to begin producing power in 1898, he offered to install two AC generators in the Railway powerhouse. The government agreed but reversed its decision the following year. Under the new terms, Canadian Niagara would still be allowed to build within the park but would have to share the river's water with competitors.

In 1901, Canadian Niagara finally began building its power station on Cedar Island, fifteen hundred feet above the Horseshoe. The river was blocked behind the island to form an ice-free fore bay. Steel penstocks ten feet in diameter conducted the water to a pair of generators 136 feet underground, and a tunnel twenty-two hundred feet long returned it to the river below the falls (the outlet is near the "Journey Behind the Falls" observation decks).

The plant opened on January 2, 1905. It began transmitting power to Fort Erie two years later, and by 1927, all eleven generators were online.

That same year, the Canadian Niagara Power Generating Station was renamed after William Birch Rankine. A founder of both Canadian Niagara and the Niagara Falls Power Company—and an officer of many other companies operating around the falls—Rankine had died in September, 1905, just forty-seven years old (Albert Duane Shaw had died in 1901, at the age of 61).

The **Ontario Power Company** built its generating station at the foot of the cliff, below Queen Victoria Park. I took this picture in the late 1990s, when the plant was still in operation (and before the high-rise hotels were built).

BROTHERS LUCIAN AND PAUL NUNN settled in Telluride, Colorado in 1880. They practiced law and sold real estate, founded the First National Bank of Telluride, and ran the nearby Gold King Mine. In 1890, Lucian started the Telluride Power Company and worked with George Westinghouse to build the Ames Hydroelectric Generating Plant. By the following summer, the plant was supplying alternating current to the machinery at the goldmine. Over the next decade, the brothers invested heavily in hydro power; to train a workforce, they built the Telluride Institute in Utah.

The abandoned **Ontario Power Company** station photographed from Niagara Falls State Park in 2013.

The brothers came to Niagara Falls in 1899 and chartered the Ontario Power Company. When the plant opened in 1905, Paul Nunn published an account of its construction, based on a talk he gave before the American Institute of Electrical Engineers. He described the powerhouse, which sat at the bottom of the gorge, as "a long but unobtrusive building ... of modest though massive design ... its colors almost blend with those of the overhanging cliff." Because of the limited space on the riverbank, the building was a thousand feet long but only seventy-six feet wide; inside was a row of fifteen generators. The distributing station was built on top of the cliff, a building "less massive but more ornate," Nunn wrote, "which on account of its commanding position is by far the most prominent landmark of the Canadian side."

Water was drawn from a bay a mile above the falls. "On account of its location in the public park," Nunn wrote, "the top of the long, narrow screen-house, approached at either end by broad steps and landings, is finished as a promenade" offering "superb views of the upper rapids." Buried conduits fed the water to six penstocks, each six feet in diameter and tunneled behind the gorge wall.

The Ontario Power Company's generating station remained in use until 1999, but its location was not always ideal. Ice flooded the plant in 1909, and again in 1938, shutting it down for several months each time.

TORONTO BUSINESSMEN Frederic Nicholls, William McKenzie, and Henry Pellatt chartered the Electrical Development Company of Ontario in February 1903, to supply power to Toronto. Nicholls published magazines and newspapers, including Toronto's *Evening Sun*, and in 1892, he organized Canadian General Electric. McKenzie owned the Toronto Railway and the Canadian Northern, and Pellatt was a stockbroker. After obtaining a license from the Niagara Parks Commission, they hired Toronto architect Edward James Lennox to design a Renaissance-styled powerhouse; as Nicholls explained in his book *Niagara's Power*:

> The Park Commissioners ... have been rigidly insistent upon the various works of construction being so planned that when completed they will not only not detract from the physical beauty of their surroundings, but add ... monuments of engineering skill and modern achievement...

The imposing ruins of the Electrical Development Company's
Toronto Power House, photographed from Goat Island.

Completed in 1906, Electrical Development's Toronto
Power House was both. Built up from the riverbed, in what
Nicholls called "the most turbulent part of the upper rapids,"
it was 467 feet long and ninety-one feet wide. A wing dam 735
feet long diverted water into the penstocks, which fed eleven
turbines. From the bottom of this wheel pit, 150 feet
underground, a stone-faced tunnel two thousand feet long
carried the spent water to an outlet behind the Horseshoe.

On the grounds facing the Canadian shoreline, "broad
terraces," Nicholls wrote, "enhanced here and there with
parapets and wide flights of steps will be constructed..."

A wide colonnade, supported by massive stone columns, graces the entire front of the structure, and from this colonnade visitors will be able to view, through large plate glass windows, the complete operation of the massive machinery within the building.

ADAM BECK WAS BORN IN BADEN, Ontario in 1857; his father had founded the village three years earlier, naming it after the German town his own parents had emigrated from in 1829. After working a few years in his father's foundry, which produced iron for the nearby Grand Trunk Railway, Adam joined his brother William in running a cigar-box factory. By 1885, they had moved the company to London, Ontario, where Adam Beck became interested in civic improvement and politics. He founded the London Health Association (now University and Victoria Hospitals) in 1900, and the Queen Alexandra Sanitorium in 1909 (today it is the London Child and Parent Resource Institute). As a member of the growing Conservative Party, he won a seat on the Ontario Legislature and was elected mayor of London three times (1902-04).

Like many municipal leaders, Beck mistrusted the Niagara Falls electric companies. Two were owned by foreign investors. All overcharged for their power, and in the race to electrify Toronto and Buffalo, they were bypassing many smaller communities. Arguing that, "the gifts of nature are for the public," Beck convinced Ontario's new Premier, Sir James Whitney, that the electrical grid should be publicly owned.

On June 7, 1906, Whitney appointed Adam Beck chairman of the new Hydro-Electric Power Commission of Ontario. Against the opposition of the power company owners, the Commission began building transmission lines and regulating

146

rates. An 110,000-volt line to Toronto, started in 1908, was turned on in 1910. By 1914, the Commission was serving a hundred cities and towns, many of which had been added to the grid with publicity-generating "turning on" celebrations.

Knighted by King George V in June 1914, Sir Adam Beck soon announced even bigger plans for the Hydro-Electric Commission: instead of just buying and distributing power, he felt the Commission should generate it as well. The public agreed, so in 1917, the Commission bought the Ontario Power Company and its riverfront powerhouse; four years later, it acquired the Electrical Development Company's Toronto Power Station.

The biggest part of Beck's plan was a new generating station, designed and built by the Commission to make the most efficient use of Niagara's water. The farther water fell on its way to the turbines, the more power it generated. Build a plant in Queenston, on the edge of the Niagara Escarpment, and water drawn from above the falls would drop more than three hundred feet.

The project was approved by a public vote on January 1, 1917, and construction of a twelve-mile canal began that May. To feed water into the canal, workers began widening and deepening the first four miles of the Welland River, which used to flow into the Niagara above Navy Island; when the work was done, water poured from the Niagara into the Welland. The canal was filled with water on Christmas Eve, 1921; one month later, the first two generators at the new Queenston-Chippawa Power Station were turned on.

The **Sir Adam Beck Generating Stations** are located in Queenston, Ontario, across the river from the New York Power Authority's Robert Moses Generating Station (photographed from the Power Vista).

By 1930, all ten generators were installed. Each was supplied by a concrete-encased penstock, sixteen feet in diameter and 383 feet long. The entire station was 590 feet long, 135 wide, and generated more than four hundred thousand kilowatts. In 1950 it was renamed after Sir Adam Beck, who had died in 1925 of anemia.

Following the passage of the 1950 Niagara Diversion Treaty, the Hydro-Electric Commission began building another station at Queenston, south of the first. The sixteen generators, driven by water falling 292 feet through concrete and steel penstocks sixteen feet in diameter, were turned on between 1954 and 1958. Called Sir Adam Beck II, the plant is 875 feet long and uses three times as much water as its older neighbor.

The Toronto Power Station was shut down in 1973, the Ontario Power Generating Station in 1999 (the riverbank powerhouse sits abandoned, but the distribution building on top of the cliff has been incorporated into the government-run Casino Niagara). The Rankine Generating Station was decommissioned last. In 2009, it was given—with all its machinery intact—to the Niagara Parks Commission, which plans to maintain it as a historic site.

The water allowances for these three plants were transferred to the Sir Adam Beck Generating Stations. All the generators in Sir Adam Beck I were upgraded in the first decade of the present century. And in March, 2013, Ontario Power Generation—a modern descendent of Beck's Hydro-Electric Commission—completed the six-mile Niagara Tunnel Project, which redirected the water that had driven the older plants to the Adam Beck stations, increasing their output by 150 megawatts.

Chapter Sixteen
Bridging the Whirlpool Rapids

ENGINEER CHARLES ELLET, JR. built the Niagara River's first suspension bridge in 1848. It crossed a mile and a half below the falls, where the gorge was eight hundred feet across—the narrowest spot from which the falls could be seen.

The bridge was the dream of Canadian businessman and politician William Hamilton Merritt. Like many colonists who sided with the British during the Revolution, Merritt's father had moved his family to Canada in the late 1700s. During the War of 1812, William Merritt patrolled the Canadian side of the river and fought in several battles.

After peace was restored, Merritt started several successful businesses, including a grist mill, a salt works, and a distillery. In 1824, he chartered a company to build a shipping canal across the Niagara Peninsula, and sold bonds to finance its construction.

Before this canal opened in 1829, ships had to be unloaded above Niagara Falls. Their cargoes were hauled down the steep Portage Road to the docks at Queenston, where they were reloaded onto ships bound for Montreal. Merritt's Welland Canal (named for the Ontario River which supplied its water) raised or lowered ships from one lake to the other—a total of 326.5 feet—using a series of forty wooden locks. Rebuilt and enlarged several times, with the number of locks gradually reduced to eight, the canal is still in operation.

Merritt was elected to Canada's Legislative Assembly in 1832 and would remain a member until 1860. He decided to build a suspension bridge across the Niagara in 1844, after reading a letter from his sons. Writing from Switzerland, they described the suspension bridge that had been built ten years before over the Sarine River at Fribourg. By 1846, Merritt was on the board of directors of the Niagara Falls Suspension Bridge Company.

Four engineers submitted designs. The two most experienced were Charles Ellet and John A. Roebling. Samuel Keefer had just begun his bridge building career, and Edward Serrell, who had proposed a Niagara suspension bridge a few years earlier—when he was nineteen—had yet to build a major bridge.

Ellet studied in Paris at the *École Nationale des Ponts et Chaussées* (National School of Bridges and Roadways; the world's first engineering school, it was founded in 1747, and is now part of the Paris Institute of Technology). He worked as a surveyor and assistant engineer on the Chesapeake and Ohio Canal, and built the United States' first cable suspension bridge in 1842, over the Schuylkill River in Fairmount, Pennsylvania. (Fairmount is now part of Philadelphia. Ellet's bridge replaced "The Colossus," a wooden bridge built in 1812 and destroyed by fire in 1838. It was replaced in 1875, and again in 1965.)

The first **Niagara Falls Suspension Bridge,** seen from the north with the falls in the background (1848 illustration by Charles Parson).

The company directors found Ellet's plans more conservative than Roebling's and awarded him a contract to build a pedestrian and carriage bridge in November 1847. Because the bridge would cross the Niagara's most dangerous rapids, getting the first cable across took some ingenuity. No ice bridge would form here; no boat could cross this part of the river.

Ellet briefly considered shooting a line across with a rocket, but decided in January, 1848 to use a kite instead. For publicity's sake, he announced a contest, with a five-dollar prize for the first person to fly a kite across the gorge and land it on the opposite cliff.

Like many local boys, fifteen-year-old Homan Walsh crossed the river to the Canadian side, where the winds were more favorable. After a day and a night of trying, he landed his kite on the American cliff, only to see the line catch on the rocks and snap. He did not get to try again until more than a week later. Ice had filled the river below the falls, grounding the ferry and stranding him on the Canadian shore (luckily, he had friends there to stay with). When he finally got back to New York, Walsh found and repaired his kite, then took it back to Canada for a second try. This time he succeeded. His kite-string was tied to a tree and used to haul a heavier rope between the shores.

By March, Ellet had passed a wire cable seven-eighths of an inch in diameter and twelve hundred feet long across the gorge. From this, he hung an iron basket, which could be pulled across with ropes and pulleys (it now hangs from the ceiling of the Buffalo History Museum). After his first crossing, Ellet told reporters:

> The wind was high and the weather cold, but yet the trip was a very interesting one to me—perched up as I was two hundred and forty feet above the rapids, and viewing from the center of the river one of the sublimest prospects which nature has prepared on this globe of ours.

The basket was built to carry workers and supplies, but Ellet also put it to work as a tourist attraction. On busy days, up to 125 visitors paid a dollar each for the short ride across the gorge and back.

Despite these distractions, the bridge was built quickly. Four wooden towers, each eighty feet tall, carried the heavy suspension cables. The oak roadway was completed in July, and Ellet made the first crossing in a horse-drawn carriage on the twenty-ninth, two days before the official opening.

This first bridge over the rapids was never meant to be permanent. Ellet intended using it as scaffolding for a larger and sturdier structure, with carriage lanes and pedestrian walks on either side of a railroad track. But before he could start this expansion, he had a falling out with the company directors and left to work fulltime on another suspension bridge in Wheeling, West Virginia.

Ellet and Roebling had both submitted designs for a suspension bridge over the Ohio River in 1847. Ellet proposed building the world's longest suspension span, more than a thousand feet. Roebling submitted a more conservative design, with a shorter span supported by two stone piers in the river. Ellet's plan was chosen because the city's businessmen feared that Roebling's piers would obstruct shipping.

In 1854, five years after the Wheeling Bridge opened, a windstorm destroyed the wooden deck. Ellet salvaged the wreckage and rebuilt, adding additional cables to stiffen the span. Declared a National Historic Landmark in 1975, the bridge now carries two car lanes on a steel grate deck.

Early in the Civil War, Ellet converted four Mississippi steamboats into unarmed rams for the Union Navy. Supported by five Union gunboats, they engaged eight Confederate warships near Memphis on June 6, 1862. Commanding his boats separately from the rest of the Union force, Ellet disabled the *CSS Colonel Lovell* by ramming it with his *Queen of the West*. Ellet's vessel was then struck by a Confederate ram, and he was shot in the knee. The Union won the battle, capturing or destroying all but one of the Confederates, but Ellet contracted measles in the field hospital and died on June 21, 1862.

JOHN AUGUSTUS ROEBLING was born in 1806, in the medieval Prussian town of Mülhuasen. He earned an engineering degree in Berlin, but soon tired of building military roads and moved to Pennsylvania. He founded the farming town of Germania (now Saxonburg) in 1831 and became an American citizen six years later. Unsuccessful at farming, Roebling quickly returned to engineering. He worked on several of Pennsylvania's canals and railroads, and began manufacturing wire rope in 1841, after witnessing a fatal accident on the Allegheny Portage Railroad. The Portage was part of the Pennsylvania Mainline Canal, built between 1828 and 1835 to connect Philadelphia and Pittsburgh. Canal boats were hauled over the Allegheny Mountains in specially built railcars, which were pulled up inclined planes with hemp ropes; Roebling saw two men die after one of those ropes snapped.

Roebling designed his first suspension bridge—a wooden canal aqueduct over the Allegheny River at Pittsburgh—in 1844. He built the city's first highway suspension bridge two years later, and a second in 1859. Unfortunately, they are all gone; the Pennsylvania Mainline Canal closed in 1901, and the highway bridges were long ago replaced.

The oldest surviving Roebling bridge was built in 1849, as an aqueduct for the Delaware and Hudson Canal. Restored by the National Park Service in the 1980s, it now carries cars and pedestrians across the Delaware River, between Lackawaxen, Pennsylvania and Minisink Ford, New York. The original wire ropes are mostly concealed by the wooden sidewalls.

In 1851, the directors of the Niagara Falls Suspension Bridge Company hired Roebling to complete their gorge crossing. Instead of placing rails and carriage lanes on a single wide deck, as Ellet intended, Roebling designed a double-decked wooden bridge. The upper deck would carry trains, the lower carriages and pedestrians. Wooden trusses would connect the decks, stiffening the bridge so it could survive heavy winds.

Two pairs of limestone towers and four wire cables supported the bridge. The towers were eighty-eight feet tall on the American side, ten feet shorter on the Canadian. Their foundations were dug twenty-eight feet deep. Each cable—ten and a half inches in diameter and spun from more than three thousand wires—was secured to a wrought iron plate six feet square, which was buried at least twenty feet deep in bedrock. The wooden bridge hung from steel cables attached to the suspension cables. Diagonal guy lines stretched from the upper deck to the tops of the towers; additional guys were added in 1854, following the collapse of Ellet's Wheeling Suspension Bridge.

The upper deck carried four rails, spaced to form three overlapping tracks of separate gauges, one for each of the roads crossing the bridge: The Great Western, the New York Central, and the New York and Erie. The bridge officially opened on March 18, 1855, though the lower deck had already been in use for several months.

A town called Suspension Bridge grew up around the eastern end of the span, complete with hotels and tourist attractions. The U.S. Customs House was moved there from Lewiston in 1863, when the bridge was carrying up to forty-five trains daily. Suspension Bridge was incorporated into the new City of Niagara Falls in 1892.

Roebling's **Niagara Falls Suspension Bridge** is featured in this 1876 Great Western Railway advertisement by William Edgard.

In the summer of 1869, John Augustus Roebling visited the site of the future Brooklyn Bridge. He lost several toes when a docking ferry crushed his right foot, and he died three weeks later of tetanus. His son Washington completed the bridge in 1883. Another son, Carl, built a cable mill south of Trenton and founded the Village of Roebling, New Jersey; the Main Gate Building is now the Roebling Museum.

AS TRAINS GREW HEAVIER and the damp Niagara weather took its toll on Roebling's wooden decks and trusses, critics began questioning the safety of the Suspension Bridge. In 1877, the owners hired engineer Leffert L. Buck was to replace all of the wood with iron—a job he completed in 1880, without interrupting traffic. When he finished rebuilding the towers in 1886, all that remained of Roebling's bridge were the cables.

This photograph of the nearly completed **Whirlpool Rapids Bridge** was first printed in the 1898 *Transactions of the American Society of Civil Engineers*.

Even rebuilt of iron, the Suspension Bridge was soon considered obsolete. Buck began building a steel arch underneath it in April 1896. He then built an iron double-decker around Roebling's structure, and—again without interrupting rail service—disassembled the older bridge. Completed on August 27, 1897, this bridge is still in service, carrying both trains and passenger cars. Long known as the Lower Steel Arch Bridge, it was renamed the Whirlpool Rapids Bridge in 1937.

Did you know?

The speed limit for trains on Roebling's wooden bridge was five miles per hour. They were not permitted to cross at full speed until Buck finished the arch bridge.

The **Whirlpool Rapids Bridge**, photographed from the American rim, looking south. The elevated portion of the Robert Moses Parkway can be seen at the upper left.

Leffert Lefferts Buck left his engineering studies in 1861 to enlist in the Union Army and fight at Antietam, Chancellorsville, and Gettysburg. He completed his degree in 1868 and built the world's highest railroad bridge five years later, for the Lima and Oroya railroad in Peru. His final work, the Williamsburg Bridge over New York's East River, opened in 1903. Its sixteen-hundred-foot suspension span remained the world's-longest until 1924, when the Bear Mountain Bridge was built over the Hudson River.

The Michigan Central Railroad Bridge

IN THE FIRST HALF of the nineteenth century, Cornelius Vanderbilt created a steamship empire and amassed one of America's largest fortunes (to celebrate his success, he awarded himself the title of "Commodore"). He began buying railroads in the 1860s, eventually combining many smaller lines into the mighty New York Central. To control the shortest route between New York and Chicago, Vanderbilt bought the Michigan Central and a controlling interest in the Canada Southern, both of which crossed the Niagara Gorge on Roebling's suspension bridge.

The Commodore died in 1877. By 1882, his heirs had decided they were paying too much to use the Suspension Bridge. In December, they asked German-born engineer Charles Conrad Schneider to design a new span, to be built south of Roebling's.

Educated at Germany's Royal School of Technology, Schneider had settled in the United States in 1867. After four years at New Jersey's Paterson Locomotive Works, he moved to Detroit to work for the Michigan Bridge and Construction Company. In 1877, he completed a twenty-three-span bridge across the Susquehanna River for the Pennsylvania Railroad (the present bridge at this location, completed in 1902, has forty-eight stone arches).

To carry the Michigan Central across the Niagara, Schneider designed one of the world's first railroad cantilever bridges. There would be two cantilever sections, each 325 feet long, each supported by a steel tower rising 132.5 feet from the riverbank. One end of each section would be attached to the gorge rim; the other would hang over the rapids.

The **Niagara Cantilever Bridge** and the Whirlpool Rapids Bridge photographed from the American shore looking north. (Detroit Publishing Company, c. 1920)

The railroad directors approved Schneider's plans in April 1883, but wanted the bridge completed by November first—an impossible deadline that Buffalo's Central Bridge Works missed by only one month. The towers were completed on October 11, the cantilevers November 18. Three days later, a steel truss was fitting into the 120-foot gap between the outer ends of the cantilevers.

To test the strength of the new bridge, the Michigan Central assembled two trains of loaded freight cars. Each was as long as the bridge, and when they crossed simultaneously, one from each end, they completely filled the two tracks. Ten thousand people gathered to watch the test. The bridge was declared safe and would carry Michigan Central trains for the next forty-two years.

In 1924, the Michigan Central began building a steel arch bridge one hundred feet north of the cantilever. After the single-track span opened in 1925, the older bridge was closed and sold for scrap. Unless it can be preserved as a historic structure, the arch bridge—closed in 1999 to remove rail traffic from the tourist section of Niagara Falls, Ontario—may soon suffer the same fate.

Did you know?

Charles Conrad Schneider submitted plans for a steel arch bridge over New York's Harlem River, connecting Manhattan to The Bronx, in 1885. Though his design was simplified to cut costs, the Washington Bridge—opened to pedestrians in 1888 and to carriages the following year—was placed on the National Register of Historic Places in 1982. It now carries six automobile lanes.

The **Michigan Central Railroad Bridge** photographed from the New York side of the Niagara Gorge. The barriers were installed when the bridge was closed in 1999.

Chapter Seventeen
Lewiston and Queenston

THE FRENCH ESTABLISHED a trading post at the foot of the Niagara Escarpment in 1719. Called the Landing, it marked the beginning of the portage road up the escarpment and around the falls and rapids. The British took over in 1759, and in 1764, military engineer John Montressor built America's first railway—The Old Lewiston Incline—to pull fully loaded wagons from the Landing up a wooden road to the top of the cliff.

During and after the American Revolution, many Loyalists crossed the Niagara River to the Canadian shore. The small town that sprang up opposite the Landing was named "Queenston" in the 1790s, after the Queen's Rangers, the military regiment that had its barracks there.

On the American side of the river, a small town was laid out in 1805 and named after New York Governor Morgan Lewis. Ten numbered streets ran parallel to the river, and the first six cross streets were named after the Six Nations of the Iroquois Confederacy: Mohawk, Oneida, Onondaga, Cayuga, Seneca, and Tuscarora.

The **Lewiston Museum**, built in the 1830s as Saint Paul's Episcopal Church, was an important stop on the "Underground Railroad" of the 1850s.

Brock's Monument, overlooking the Niagara River from Queenston Heights, was dedicated on October 13, 1859. The 185-foot limestone shaft replaced an earlier monument to Major General Isaac Brock, which was partly destroyed by an anti-British bomber in 1840.

Early on the morning of October 13, 1812, American soldiers and New York militia gathered at Lewiston to invade Canada. Though the British artillery on Queenston Heights splashed eighteen-pound balls into the river, enough Americans landed to capture the hilltop battery. Major General Isaac Brock, in command of British Army troops, Canadian militia, and three hundred Mohawk warriors, led the charge to recapture Queenston Heights. Though he died in the attempt, his successor—Major General Roger Hale Sheaffe—surrounded the American forces late in the afternoon and accepted their surrender.

In December 1813, British forces attacked Lewiston. Overwhelmed, the militia fled, leaving the townspeople undefended. In retaliation for the burning of Newark, a Canadian town on the shore of Lake Ontario, the British and their native allies set Lewiston ablaze. They might also have killed everyone there, but for the intervention of a small force of Tuscarora. The Indians held the soldiers at bay until the townspeople escaped, and then gave the Americans food and shelter while Lewiston was rebuilt.

After the war, Lewiston and Queenston resumed their lives as busy river ports (the British had built docks and a new portage road on the Canadian side in the 1790s). In the 1820s, Lewiston was still a bigger city than Buffalo, with fine hotels and a United States Customs House. Business dried up in the 1830s, after the Erie and Welland Canals made the portage roads unnecessary.

In the 1850s, Lewiston became an important stop on the "Underground Railroad." The passage of the Fugitive Slave Act in 1850 meant it was no longer enough for escaped slaves to run north; if they hoped to stay free, they needed to leave the United States. Lewiston citizens, including tailor Josiah Tryon, hid fugitives in their homes and in Saint Paul's Episcopal and The First Presbyterian Churches until they could be rowed across to Canada after dark. (Other "conductors" on the Underground Railroad rowed escaped slaves to Fort Erie from Buffalo or smuggled them across the lower level of Roebling's suspension bridge.)

Children's author Margaret Goff Clark, who lived near Lewiston, presented a fictionalized account of these events in her 1969 novel *Freedom Crossing*. Still in print, the book is used in many fourth- and fifth-grade classrooms to introduce students to the Underground Railroad.

On October 14, 2009, the Lewiston Historical Society unveiled the Freedom Crossing Monument on the Lewiston waterfront. Sculpted by artist Susan Geissler and cast in bronze, the monument includes larger-than-life figures of Josiah Tryon and Laura Eastman, the teenaged heroine of *Freedom Crossing* (she is pointing across the river to Canada).

Visitors to Lewiston's 1824 **Frontier House** hotel included Mark Twain, Charles Dickens, Washington Irving, the Marquis de Lafayette, New York Governor DeWitt Clinton, President William McKinley, and King Edward VII. Abandoned since 2004, the Frontier now belongs to the Town of Lewiston, which plans to restore it as a historic attraction (its Center Street neighbors include a variety of restaurants, shops, and galleries).

The **Freedom Crossing Monument** by Susan Geissler. Laura Eastman, the heroine of Margaret Goff Clark's novel *Freedom Crossing*, points across the river to Canada, while real-life Underground Railroad conductor Josiah Tryon hands a child to the woman in the rowboat.

Another work by Susan Geissler, the Tuscarora Heroes Monument, *was unveiled in Lewiston on December 19, 2013—the two-hundredth anniversary of the burning of the village during the War of 1812.*

The **Niagara River,** looking north from the Lewiston docks.

Did you know?

Governor Morgan Lewis had served as a quartermaster during the American Revolution and was promoted to major general during the War of 1812. On March 2, 1813, he led the American force that captured Fort George, on the Lake Ontario shoreline across the river from Fort Niagara. His father, New York merchant Francis Lewis, signed both the Declaration of Independence and the Articles of Confederation. Morgan's wife, Gertrude, was the daughter of Robert Livingston, the powerful New York landowner and politician who financed Robert Fulton's steamboat experiments (Fulton's *Clermont* was named after Livingston's Hudson River estate).

The **Lewiston-Queenston Bridge** photographed from the visitors' center at the New York Power Project. The buildings on the left are part of Canada's Sir Adam Beck Generating Station.

The Lewiston-Queenston Bridge

IN 1850, EDWARD SERRELL won the contract to build a suspension bridge between Queenston, Ontario and Lewiston, New York (Charles Ellet, Jr. and John A. Roebling had also submitted designs). A steamboat towed the first cable across the Niagara—there were no rapids this far downriver—and the wooden roadway opened for carriage and pedestrian traffic on March 20, 1851.

Serrell anchored iron stays to both shorelines, to stiffen the bridge in heavy winds. Afraid that river ice would damage these stays, the bridge's owners had them disconnected in January

1864. Early that February, a windstorm ripped through the gorge and destroyed the road deck. Though the four masonry towers and the iron cables survived, the deck was never rebuilt; for the next thirty-five years, a steam ferry carried passengers across this part of the river.

During the Civil War, Serrell raised the First New York Volunteer Engineer Regiment and designed batteries for the siege of Charleston. In 1868, he chartered the Hudson Highland Suspension Bridge Company to build a double-decked railroad and wagon bridge at Bear Mountain. Unable to secure funding, he abandoned this project when the Poughkeepsie Railroad Bridge opened in 1888.

The ruined Queenston-Lewiston span was finally removed in 1898. After completing the Lower Steel Arch Bridge, Leffert L. Buck supervised the disassembly of the second Falls View Suspension Bridge. He then moved the cables and eight hundred tons of steel parts to Lewiston, to build a new suspension bridge to Canada. Opened in July 1899, it remained in service until November 1962.

By the 1950s, leaders on both sides of the river were talking about replacing the suspension bridge. Robert Moses, chairman of the New York State Power Authority, included a new bridge in his 1956 plans for the massive hydroelectric plant at Lewiston (these plans also included a still-controversial parkway along the American rim of the gorge).

Engineer Henry Wallace Fisher modeled the new crossing after the Rainbow Bridge. The steel arch was the largest in the world, a thousand feet across—fifty feet longer than the Rainbow Bridge, and almost twice as high; the top of the arch is 370 feet above the river.

Located seven-tenths of a mile south of the suspension bridge, the Lewiston-Queenston Bridge opened on November 1, 1962. The old bridge was closed the following day, and then dismantled and sold for scrap in March 1963.

Did you know?

The four stone towers that supported Edward Serrell's suspension bridge can still be seen in their original locations. The Canadian towers are in York Park, the American in the Earl V. Brydges Artpark. Built on the site of a former industrial waste dump in Lewiston, New York, the Artpark has an art gallery, a theater, and a ten-thousand seat outdoor amphitheater. Follow the  trail uphill past these to find sculptor Owen Morrel's *Omega*, a stairway and observation deck supported by the two old towers. (The stairway was closed when I visited, the deck home to at least a dozen turkey buzzards.)

Built in the 1960s, the eighteen-mile **Robert Moses State Parkway** has long been condemned as a barrier between the city and the riverfront, and a major cause of Niagara Falls' urban blight. A short section that crossed Niagara Falls State Park was removed in the 1980s, and in 2001, three miles of the southbound lanes were closed to motor traffic and renamed "The Robert Moses Recreational Trail." In February 2013, the State of New York announced plans to remove the two-mile stretch beginning north of the Rainbow Bridge and replace it with parklands. (The demolition had not yet begun in September 2013, when I took this photograph of the elevated section overlooking the Whirlpool Rapids bridges.)

Chapter Eighteen
Old Fort Niagara

BETWEEN 1679 AND 1826, three nations vied for control of the Niagara Portage. The French arrived first. Explorer Étienne Brûlé is credited with discovering Lakes Erie, Ontario, Huron, and Superior. He was also the first European to learn the Huron language, and was probably the first to see the Niagara River (Samuel de Champlain, to whom Brûlé reported at Quebec, included the Niagara on his 1632 map of the region, but never saw it himself).

In 1679, La Salle built a fortified storehouse—grandly named "Fort Conti" after his lieutenant's patron—where the Niagara empties into Lake Ontario. The Iroquois had given him (and by extension, France) permission to use the Niagara Portage; it was not a right he intended to share with the British, who had taken New Amsterdam from the Dutch in 1664. Fire claimed the wooden fort in less than a year, and the site was abandoned until 1687.

Jacques Rene de Brisay—the Marquis de Denonville— served as Governor General of New France from 1685 until 1689. Relations between the French and the Iroquois had deteriorated, so Denonville tried—unsuccessfully, of course—to drive the Indians from the Niagara Peninsula. To control the Portage, he had Fort Denonville built in 1687, on the site of La Salle's Fort Conti.

In a single harsh winter, disease and starvation killed all but a dozen of the fort's defenders. Before the stockade was abandoned in the spring, Chaplain Pierre Millet raised an eighteen-foot wooden cross on the lakeshore in memory of the dead.

Less trusting than they had been in La Salle's day, the Iroquois refused to allow another fort at the mouth of the Niagara. In 1719, they let Louis-Thomas Chabert de Joncaire build a small trading post at the foot of the portage trail, in modern-day Lewiston. (Taken captive by the Seneca as a young man, Chabert had won their trust and respect, and spent the rest of his life as an interpreter and diplomat.) Five years later, Chabert convinced the Iroquois to allow the construction of a stone trading post where Forts Conti and Denonville had once stood.

Completed in 1727, Chabert's new "House of Peace" was a fort in everything but name. Though one small room on the first floor was in fact used as a trading post, the rest of the stone building was designed to house sixty soldiers and their officers. Before long, it was known as "Fort Niagara," and when the French and Indian War broke out in the 1750s, the French reinforced their "trading post" with earthworks.

The British arrived in July 1759, surrounding Fort Niagara with 2,400 soldiers and a thousand Iroquois warriors. Day by day they moved closer, digging trenches toward the earthworks. Inside, the fort's six hundred French defenders waited for a promised relief force.

At **Fort Niagara**, the British built two stone "redoubts"—self-contained forts that could be held even if the main walls were overrun—in the 1770s (I took this photograph of the North Redoubt from the upper level of the South Redoubt, through which visitors enter the restored fort). The Knights of Columbus dedicated the eighteen-foot bronze cross on the lakeshore in 1926, in memory of the cross Father Millet built in 1788.

July 24, the relief force collided with British troops a mile south of Fort Niagara and was defeated. The following day, Captain Pierre Pouchot surrendered the fort.

During the Revolution, the British sent raiding parties out from Fort Niagara to harass American frontier settlements. And although the war ended in 1783, the British held their western forts another thirteen years, finally turning Fort Niagara over to the American Army in 1796. By 1799, the

British had completed Fort George, facing Fort Niagara across the broad mouth of the river.

Relations between the American and British troops stationed on the frontier remained friendly until 1812. In October, the garrisons at Forts Niagara and George shelled each other during the Battle of Queenston Heights. In November, the Americans removed the roof of the old "House of Peace" to make room for a gun deck from which they could fire down into Fort George.

The British abandoned Fort George in May 1813. American forces held it until December, when militia General George McClure decided to return his men to Fort Niagara. Before leaving, he gave orders to destroy the fort and burn the lakeshore town of Newark.

The British retaliation was swift and brutal. With their Mohawk allies, they stormed Fort Niagara on December 19, and then burned most of the American settlements along the Niagara.

A year later, on Christmas Eve, the war was declared over. Neither could really claim victory; the Treaty of Ghent restored all the pre-war borders. In May, American troops returned to Fort Niagara.

With the opening of the Erie Canal in 1825, business dwindled on the Niagara Portage. Cargos that once had to be unloaded, carried around the falls and rapids, and then reloaded onto ships for the long voyage across Lake Ontario and down the Saint Lawrence River could now cross New York State on towboats to the Hudson. In 1826, Fort Niagara was abandoned.

Three flags fly in front of Fort Niagara's 1727 **French Castle**. On the left is the plain white flag of the French Navy, on the right the British Union Jack. The American flag in the center has fifteen stars and fifteen stripes; a much larger version, which flew over Fort Niagara during the War of 1812, can be seen in the visitor's center. (The most famous flag of this design is the "Star Spangled Banner" displayed at the Smithsonian, the flag that inspired our national anthem by surviving the British shelling of Baltimore's Fort McHenry in September 1814.)

Edward Giddings, a local innkeeper and ferry operator, was appointed caretaker. For two years he looked after the empty fort. Every night, he climbed the stairs to light the nine whale oil lamps in the rooftop lighthouse.

The British had first placed a lantern on top of Chabert's "French Castle" in 1781. The American government removed it in 1803, after the British built a new lighthouse at Fort George (called the Newark Light, it was demolished in 1814).

Congress voted to replace the Fort Niagara light in 1823, and had a new tower and lantern built on top of the Castle.

In 1829, Giddings published an account describing his part in one of the strangest events in the fort's long history. Three years earlier, Freemason William Morgan had vanished from nearby Batavia, New York, after threatening to reveal the society's secrets. Giddings, who was also a Mason, claimed that Morgan was abducted by fellow Masons, imprisoned for several days in the fort's empty powder magazine, and then drowned in the Niagara River. Although nothing was ever proved—because Giddings was an atheist, he was not allowed to testify against other accused conspirators—the story spread nationwide and led to the rise of an Anti-Masonic political party.

Fort Niagara was briefly reopened in 1828, and again in 1838. After the Civil War, the Army built new barracks outside the walls. Soldiers trained there for the Spanish-American War, officers for the First World War. The older buildings were used for storage, or simply abandoned. By the 1920s, the French Castle was in ruins.

With a combination of private donations and federal money, the nonprofit Old Fort Niagara Association began restoring the Castle in 1927. The Army allowed the Association to open Old Fort Niagara as a museum in 1931, and then gave the rest of Fort Niagara to New York for a state park in 1945 (the state did not get full use of the land until after 1963, when the last military units stationed there were reassigned).

THE UNITED STATES LIGHTHOUSE BOARD improved the Fort Niagara light in 1858, by rebuilding the antiquated lantern and installing a fourth order Fresnel lens. (Lighthouse lenses were made in seven sizes, called orders. First Order lenses were the largest; mid-sized fourth order lenses were often used for river or harbor lights.) But even the updated light soon outlasted its welcome. The old tower leaked rainwater into the castle, and the keeper could only reach the lantern by climbing stairways between the army officers' bedrooms.

So, in 1871, Congress spent sixteen thousand dollars on a fifty-foot, limestone tower outside the fort's walls. Construction began in July, was halted by a harsh winter, and then resumed in the spring. When the tower was completed in June 1872, the Fresnel lens was moved from the old rooftop lantern. In 1900, the tower was raised eleven feet, increasing the light's range from ten to fifteen miles on a clear night.

The Fort Niagara Lighthouse was deactivated in 1993, when the surrounding trees began obscuring its light. The Fresnel was moved to the Old Fort Niagara visitor's center, and an automated beacon was placed on a nearby radio tower. In the summertime, visitors can climb the tower's spiral stairs to look out over the river, the fort, and Lake Ontario.

Fort Niagara Lighthouse

About the Author

KEVIN WOYCE grew up in East Rutherford, New Jersey, the eldest of fifteen siblings. A graduate of William Paterson College, he now lives in Lyndhurst, New Jersey with his wife, Carin. In addition to writing and illustrating regional history books, he lectures throughout New Jersey and southern New York on a variety of historical topics. You can find him on Facebook as *Kevin Woyce Author*, and his speaking schedule is listed at *KevinWoyce.com*.

Books by Kevin Woyce

Jersey Shore History & Facts
New Jersey State Parks: History & Facts
Lighthouses: Connecticut & Block Island
Liberty: An Illustrated History of America's Favorite Statue
Hudson River Lighthouses: An Illustrated History
Santa's Hometown
California Visions (photographs)
Powerful PowerPoint

Selected Bibliography

American Institute of Electrical Engineers. *The Niagara Falls Electrical Handbook*. Niagara Falls: George W. Davenport, 1904.

Banks, G. Linnaeus. *Blondin: His Life and Performances*. London: Routledge, Warnes, and Routledge, 1862.

Barnes, Joseph W. "The Gold Rush Journal of Thomas Evershed: Engineer, Artist, and Rochesterian." *Rochester History* (January and April, 1977).

Bigelow, Timothy. *Journal of a Tour to Niagara Falls in the Year 1805*. Boston: Press of John Milson and Sons, 1876.

Business Men's Association of Niagara Falls. *The Water Power of the Falls of Niagara Applied to Manufacturing Purposes*. Niagara Falls: The Business Men's Association, 1890.

Commissioners of the State Reservation at Niagara. *Supplemental Report*. Albany: The Argus Company, 1887.

Dow, Charles. *The State Reservation at Niagara: A History*. Albany: J.B. Lyon Company, 1914.

Eckel, Patricia M. "Historic Background at Niagara Falls: The Porters." *Res Botanica: A Missouri Botanical Garden Website* (July 22, 2003).

Hubbard, Elbert. *Power, or the Story of Niagara Falls*. East Aurora: The Roycrofters, 1914.

Hudson, Mike. "John Stedman: Coward for the Crown, Gallant Frontiersman for Bad Historians." *Niagara Falls Reporter* (December 19, 2006).

Johnson, Paul E. *Sam Patch, the famous jumper*. New York: Hill and Wang, 1992.

Kowsky, Francis. "In Defense of Niagara: Frederick Law Olmsted and the Niagara Reservation." *The Distinctive Charms of Niagara.* Lewiston: The Buscaglia-Castellani Art Gallery of Niagara University, 1985.

Koonz, J.A. *Industrial Niagara Falls Illustrated.* Niagara Falls: The Gazette Press, 1902.

Maude, John. *Visit to the Falls of Niagara in 1800.* London: Longman, Rees, Orme, Brown, and Green, 1826.

Nicholls, Frederic. *Niagara's Power: Past, Present, Prospective.* Toronto: R.G. McLean, 1905.

Nunn, P.N. *The Development of the Ontario Power Company.* Niagara Falls: The Ontario Power Company, 1905.

Porter, Peter A. *Goat Island.* Niagara Falls: Porter, 1900.

Rogers, Cleveland. "Robert Moses: An Atlantic Portrait." *The Atlantic* (February 1, 1939).

The Shredded Wheat Company. *The Wonders of Niagara.* Niagara Falls: The Shredded Wheat Co., 1914.

Welch, Thomas. *How Niagara Was Made Free: The Passage of the Niagara Reservation Act in 1885.* Buffalo: Press Union and Times, 1903.

Speech of Hon. Thomas V. Welch, of Niagara: In the Assembly of the State of New York, Friday, March 2, 1883 (Google E-book)

Williams, Edward. *Official Record of the Niagara Falls Memorial Committee.* Niagara Falls: The Niagara Falls Memorial Committee, 1924.

Young, David. *The Humbugs of Niagara Exposed.* Suspension Bridge: Young, 1884.

Made in the USA
Las Vegas, NV
10 June 2025

23472117R00105